TARBERT FISHING BOATS

1925-75

Brian Ward

British Cataloguing in Publication Data
A catalogue record for this book is available from the British Library

ISBN: 0-9542804-5-8

*

Published in Scotland by Ardminish Press, Isle of Gigha, Argyll
Tel 01583505233/227
e-mail: enquiries@ardpress.co.uk
web site: www.ardpress.co.uk

*

Front cover: A Jack Glover painting of Tarbert c. 1950. The boats are *Florentine* CN 197, *Maireared* TT 135, *and Mary Devereux* TT148

*

This book is dedicated to all the fishermen and their families, past and present; to Janet for encouraging me to realise my ambition; to Graham and Richard for assisting with the complexities of word processing and desktop publishing; to Margery Irving for introducing me to the Tarbert skiffs, and to Mum and Dad for all their love over the years. Sadly, they will never see this book.

BW

DALRIADA BOOKS FROM ARDMINISH PRESS

£12.99

THE AUTHOR

Brian Ward was born in Edinburgh in 1947, and lived at Pier Road, Tarbert in the late 1950s and early 1960s. His mother Nina's family were all brought up in the village, and his grandfather, James Irving, was headmaster of the local school.

He is married to Janet, and they have two grown up sons, Graham and Richard. Both have been involved in the word processing, the design work and the illustrations in this book.

Brian Ward qualified as a teacher in 1969, and now resides in East Ardsley, near Leeds. His interest in fishing boats dates back to his time living and spending holidays in Tarbert. During his early 'exile' in Yorkshire, his aunt, Margery Irving kept him up to date with fishing boat developments in the Loch Fyneside village, and his interest has never waned. Living far from the lochs, his desire to own a ring-netter has had to be satisfied for the time being with a beautiful scale model by J G Wood of Ayrshire. It has pride of place in the Ward family home.

CONTENTS

INTRODUCTION

Since the late 1950s, when I went to school in Tarbert, I have had a keen interest in fishing boats. I used to spend hours at the quay studying them as they prepared for a night's fishing, discharging the catch early next morning, or simply tied up at rest. I naturally favoured the Tarbert boats, but visiting vessels from Campbeltown, Carradale, Dunure, Maidens, Pittenweem, Peel and other ports generated additional enthusiasm.

Imagine my delight when a boat from Ullapool spent a couple of weeks moored over near Dickie's boatyard. A Donald Smith print of the boat, UL276, appears later in the book. The visiting ring-netters I remember well include *Maid of the Mist* CN120, *Moira* CN33, *Mary McLean* CN193, *Nobles Again* CN37, *Amalthea* CN143, *Watchful* BA124, *Britannia* BA130, and others too numerous to mention.

This book is a written and pictorial account of the ring-netters, seine-netters and prawn trawlers that were Tarbert-registered between 1925 and 1975 – the golden era of Loch Fyne fishing. Facts and figures are important, but I have tried to find out more about the boats, their owners, skippers and crews. Where possible I have included photographs, and, having never seen many of them it was wonderful to put faces to the names.

My research has been dependent on people who are listed later in the book, and I have done my best to acknowledge photographs appropriately. Some post card manufacturers have ceased trading, so obtaining copyright permission has been impossible; I therefore apologise in advance if I have fallen foul in this respect. Some sources of photographs have proved too costly to utilise, so they will remain hidden away! Fishing families from their own collections have kindly supplied a number of the pictures.

The format of the book caused me much thought, but I eventually decided to present the boats in ascending order of registration numbers. However, this method means that some of the historical flow from the 1920s to the 1970s is lost. Appendix II tries to resolve this problem by listing the Tarbert-registered boats in blocks of five-year periods. This gives a snapshot of the fleet at any given time throughout the period of the study. The boat list pages also include the years each boat was under the TT flag.

The principal aim of my research was to collect as much information as possible on each boat. Several people assisted me in this task, including Douglas McAlpine, who encouraged me from the beginning – despite my reservations. I feel that a book like this could have been better written by a Tarbert fisherman who is familiar with the subject first hand, rather than someone who, despite having a genuine interest and affection for the boats and the village, has limited primary knowledge. Alastair Parker helped me with the initial listings of the vessels, a subject he has spent many years researching. Local fishermen Robert Ross, Peter McDougall, Willie Dickson, Willie Jackson and James McNab all provided details on boats and personalities. John Crawford, of Lochgilphead, kindly contributed many photographs from his prized collection.

In general, the boats bore similarities to each other, but could be recognised by their builder's design. (Appendix III).

The sharp and strong bows and distinct cruiser sterns of James N Miller of St Monance boats made them easily distinguishable, and the *Village Belle 111* TT34/TT66 was arguably one of this yard's finest examples. The Miller company, of course, built many outstanding boats for fishing ports on both coasts of Scotland.

Neat bows and pronounced canoe sterns were symbolic of the William Weatherhead yards at Cockenzie, Port Seton and Dunbar. The lower rubbing strips on these boats finished short of the stern similar to those built by Walter Reekie of St Monance. However the Reekie sterns were more upright and solid in appearance than those of the Weatherhead boats, and their bows were usually rounded at the top.

The ringers built by James Noble of Fraserburgh had clean bows, also rounded at the top, and canoe sterns slightly more upright than the Reekie versions.

Fairlie Yacht Slip built many fine boats, and they often featured raked bows and broad sterns. On several of their vessels the lower rubbing strip stopped well short of the bow – unlike other builders – e.g. the *Fiona* CN 165, *Stella Maris* CN 158 and *Regina Maris* CN 118. This gave them a rather slab-sided appearance, and possibly made the boats look more modern than the conventional style from other yards. However, they also built along more traditional lines, like the *Silver Cloud* TT141. The Fairlie boats could also be recognised by their deep-windowed wheelhouses.

A late entrant to the craft was fishing boat builder Alexander Noble & Sons Ltd, of Girvan, Ayrshire. This firm launched almost 100 boats from the late 1940s up until the early 1990s. Their new buildings were a combination of the best design features of the time. The lovely vessels, all of which bore a carved thistle motif at the bow, were well proportioned, with solid looking wheelhouses and distinctive curved sterns. Nowadays, the firm concentrates on the construction of steel-hulled fishfarm vessels, with the thistle painted on the plating!

Looking back, it was probably good to have a bit of variety in the general design and I now closely examine photographs of these boats and appreciate their style.

The length of Tarbert boats varied from rather dumpy 40-feet-long seine-netters to the elegant 50-feet plus ring-netters, which were my favourites. At that time – in the late 1950s – most boats, old and new, were immaculately maintained with gleaming golden varnish and silver galvanised rubbing strips; complete with similarly coated coping irons and bow and stern bands. Wheelhouses, too, were varnished and, as I recall, usually left with the doors unlocked and open; how times have changed! Skilled sign-writers painted the port registration numbers white – with blue or red shading on a black backing – at the shoulder and quarter on both sides. The boat name was usually engraved in yellow or gold on shaped boards to match the beading line encircling the hull on the outer bulwarks. Later, in the 1960s, paint took over from varnish and I feel something was lost as these boats certainly looked better in their original finish. The reasons for the change from varnish to paint were both financial and time consumption, coupled with the development of modern paints.

One ringer that suited a green painted hull was the *Evelyn* TT58, a well-proportioned boat that, despite being varnished from time to time, still looked equally good in her paint coating. Almost all the white fish boats were painted black, though when new in 1960 the *Nancy Glen* TT10 was varnished, as was the *Destiny* TT42 on her launch in 1963 from the same Dickie of Tarbert boatyard. In later years, blue and red paint was used as well, and varnished hulls have all but disappeared.

I could go into even greater detail if I considered other features, such as the addition of white bow fender tyres favoured by some of the BA and CN boats, but generally ignored by the Tarbert men with the exception of the *Village Maid 11* TT25, the *Fionnaghal* TT65 and, later in her career, the *Ann Marie* TT150. The angle of their brailer poles varied, ranging from a low setting to a steep rake as displayed by the *King Fisher* TT55. The mizzenmasts differed from stout wooden affairs to rather thin tubular steel, and the aerials changed in the early 1960s from long whip types to the parallel wires stretching from high on the mizzenmast to the peak of the angled brailer, or to an upright spar rising out of the tabernacle.

Many earlier boats had a stepped deck to facilitate more headroom in the forecastle; the later, bigger vessels had sufficient inner depth and were flush decked.

Original wheelhouses were very compact – with sufficient space only for a steering wheel and compass, and one or two men. However, these increased in height and width to accommodate an ever-increasing array of fish finding and navigation equipment. I feel the first wheelhouses were a bit small in proportion to hull dimensions, but the medium-sized structures as featured in the 1940s Weatherhead and Miller boats made an ideal combination and attractive profile. The much larger designs of the 1960s and 1970s somehow spoilt the aesthetics and made some boats look top heavy. They no doubt contributed to a more pleasant working environment at sea, but did little for the overall appearance of the boats.

I make no apology for concentrating on the vessels' aesthetics, as I feel this is what makes them so special to many of us who study them. There are surely fewer better sights than a 1950s fleet of ring-netters passing the White Shore, Tarbert, making for the herring grounds on a summer evening. However, as with all things in life, the elegance and the efficiency of a fishing boat are a compromise. Crew safety, comfort, working conditions and cost effectiveness are all more important than the look of such a vessel. This opinion can be confirmed in every fishing port in the country by studying the design of modern boats. Possibly that is why the examination of earlier examples holds more interest than the present day fleet, though there are still several traditional boats around. In years to come, I may look back at the current designs and think that they were not so bad!

There is obviously much more data to be collected on the subject, but I had to draw a line at this point. I realise that information on several boats is very limited, especially the older ones, but I have endeavoured to cover a wide range of detail in this study – from dimensions, dates, name spellings, registrations and so on. If mistakes have been made then I hope no offence has been caused. Perhaps readers with more information could contact me, as I am always eager to extend my knowledge about these boats, which sadly are becoming a distant memory.

Anyway, hopefully the following pages will rekindle the memory of this very important episode of Tarbert's history. We can still see Bruce's Castle, the churches, remnants of the boatyards, the older houses and shops, The Beilding, the piers – but no old fishing boats!

FISHING BOAT DIMENSIONS EXPLAINED

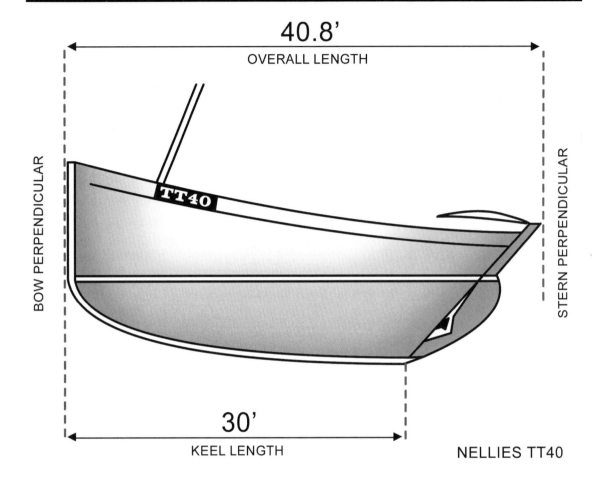

40.8'
OVERALL LENGTH

BOW PERPENDICULAR

STERN PERPENDICULAR

TT40

30'
KEEL LENGTH

NELLIES TT40

The fishing boats included in this study are all more than 30-feet-long and more then 10 tons in weight. Many older fishing skiffs were under these limits and are not represented.

At least four measurements are given for each boat at the top of its relevant section. These are length x beam x depth of hold, and the tonnage. However, the records show different methods for measuring length. The keel length, where stated, is naturally the length of the keel in feet. In the case of some boats, namely Zulu types with steeply sloping sterns, the length greatly exceeds the keel length as in the *Maggie McDougall* TT2. In fact, her length is 10 feet greater than her keel length. The registered length was measured from the perpendicular line at the stem/bow to the perpendicular line at the mid-point of the rudderstock. The overall length included the additional distance from the rudderstock to the perpendicular line at the stern. Consequently, some canoe sterned ring-net boats had a marked difference between these two measurements. For example, the *Catherine Ann* TT31, had a registered length of 52.2 feet and an overall length of 58.2 feet. In many cases only the overall length is given.

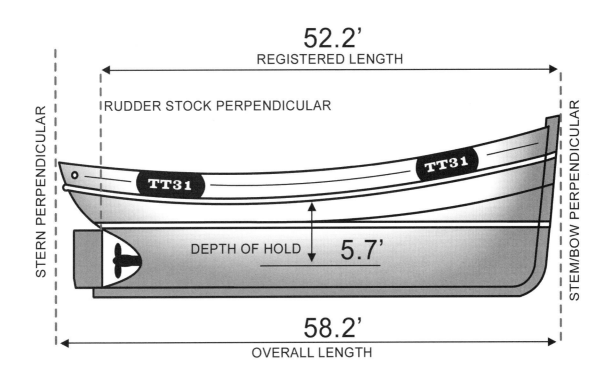

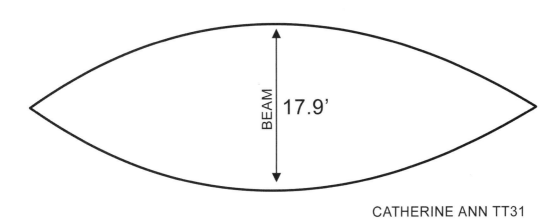

CATHERINE ANN TT31

CALCULATION OF TONNAGE

Overall length x beam x depth of hold x $\frac{0.45}{100}$ = tonnage (pre -1952)

Registered length x beam x depth of hold x $\frac{0.45}{100}$ = tonnage (post -1952)

TARBERT FISHING BOAT LIST

MAGGIE MCDOUGALL TT2...1929-1949
GLEANER TT2... 1958-1963
ENDEAVOUR TT2 1969-1973
TUDOR ROSE TT4..1968-1974
TWIN SISTERS TT8.. ?
OUR LASSIE TT8...1960-1979
NANCY GLEN (1) TT10...1939-1949
NANCY GLEN(2) TT10 / BOY JAMIE TT10.........................1960-1995
WHITE ROSE TT11...1960-1963
SALLY TT13...1902-1916
MARGARET ANN 11 TT16 1949-1954
CALEDONIA TT17..1960-1980
PROVIDER TT18.. 1969-1975
PRIDE OF THE CLYDE TT20... 1949-1952
VILLAGE MAID TT21.. 1925-1944
CATRIONA / HARMONY TT24..1969-2000
VILLAGE MAID 11 TT25...1961-1990
MARGARITA TT26.. 1961-1983
PRIME TT27..1926-1948
FAIR DAWN TT27...1970-1986
BLOSSOM TT30..1932-1942
GOLDEN GLEAM TT30... 1949-1954
GIRL MAUREEN TT30...1970-1972
CATHERINE ANN TT31...1970-2002
SEONAID TT32...1926-1953
VILLAGE BELLE TT34...1932-1945
VILLAGE BELLE 111 TT34 / TT66.............................. 1957-1970 / 1977-1994
MARY BAIN TT35 1932-1959
OSPREY TT36...1934-1958
PIONEER TT36...1971-1983
FLYING FISH TT37..1932-1947
GIRL SEONA TT37...1968-1983
NELLIES TT40..1933-1949
DESTINY TT42...1963-1985
HARMONY TT46...1963-1964
MAY TT48...1956-1959
CHARLOTTE ANN TT49...1954-1961
SMILING MORN TT50..1933-1937
MARY PAT TT52...1964-1966
KING FISHER TT55 1950-1966
UTOPIA TT55..1972-1985
MARYEARED TT57...1964-2000
EVELYN TT58...1955-1985
CATHERINE TT59..?
FIONNAGHAL (1) TT65...1934-1957
CLAN MACTAVISH TT68 / THE RANGER TT73..............1927-1937 / 1950-1992

JUNE ROSE TT68...?

SHEILA TT70 1935-1938

BOY KEN TT70..1972-1973

MARY MUNRO TT71... 1927-1950

GOLDEN WEST TT72... 1965-1970

VILLAGE BELLE 11 TT74...1940-1957

VILLAGE BELLE 1V TT74... fishing

SILVER CREST TT75...1950-1986

BELLEMAR/DALRIADA TT76 .... fishing

SILVER SPRAY TT77...1927-1939

DALRIADA TT77..1954-1978

BOY DAVID TT78... 1973-1976

TRUSTFUL 111 TT79... 1966-1967

TAEPING / CATRIONA TT79.....................................fishing

WILLING LAD TT83...1928-1940

MAISIE TT83... 1953-1964

POLLY COOK TT85...1947-1961

ISA JOHNSON TT88...1920-1940

FLORENTINE TT92...1967-1968

SILVER FERN TT93...1969-1974

JESSIE TT94...1936-1950

BOY LORNE TT94... 1967-1976

WHITE ROSE TT100... 1967-1969

MHAIREAD TT104...1957-1962

SWEET MARIE TT105...1902-1956

SCARBH TT106...1947-1951

FIONNAGHAL 11 TT106...1956-1967

TITAN TT110...1953-1964

ENDEAVOUR 11 TT112..1977-1980

MAIREARED TT113... 1938-1957

FRIGATE BIRD TT117...1947-1955

SUNBEAM TT117...1974-1995

SILVER FERN TT119... 1978-1979

OAK LEA TT131... 1947-1961

MONSOON TT132...1948-1953

LITTLE FLOWER TT134..1943-1944

MAIREARED TT135...1948-1965

CLAN MCNAB TT138...1923-1928

FAIRHAVENS TT140...1948-1954

MARGARITA TT141... 1948-1954

SILVER CLOUD / AEOLUS TT141.............................. 1977-1980

MARY DEVEREUX TT148..1949-1958

SIREADH TT150...1923-1938

ANNE MARIE TT150...1948-1984

SILVER BIRCH TT151 1949-1954

PEGGY TT334 1911-1950

THE BOATS

27' Keel
37.0 x 11 x 5.5   **10.07 tons**

The first boat in my survey is the *Maggie McDougall* TT2. She was built by the Carradale boatbuilder Matthew MacDougall at Portrigh in 1906, and became a Tarbert boat in 1929. She fished from the village until 1949, when she was sold to Kyleakin. Powered by a 22hp Kelvin diesel engine, the skiff had a wheelhouse fitted at the start of the Second World War. Her Tarbert owners were Mr Smith and Duncan McDougall (*Tar*). The *Maggie McDougall* was one of a pair known as the *Golden Swallowers* because of their fishing successes. Her neighbour for a while was the *Mary Munro* TT71.

This is an unidentified skiff – could it be the *Maggie McDougall*, the *Catherine* or the *Sally*?
(Eric Irving Collection)

39.9 x 13.3 x 4.7   15.52 tons.

The *Gleaner* was a typical 40-foot Fifie, painted black with an external rudder. J & G Forbes of Sandhaven built her in 1932, and a 66hp Kelvin engine provided power.

Previously registered in Campbeltown as CN41, the boat was owned by a Tarbert partnership comprised of Ronnie Johnson, Eoghan Smith and Willie Dickson, names we shall come across several times in this book. When she began working from Tarbert in 1958 the *Gleaner* was used as a white fish seine-netter, and also trawled for prawns. Her mast arrangement was similar to the *Our Lassie* TT8, as is shown in the photograph.

The original wheelhouse was replaced by a new one built by local joiner, Duncan McAlpine, at a cost of just £80. The *Gleaner* remained in Tarbert for five years, and was sold following the launch of the *Destiny* TT42 in 1963.

The *Gleaner* looking freshly painted, coming into Tarbert past the Point.
(Jessie Bain Collection)

39.9 x 12.0 x 4.3   **9.3 tons**

The *Endeavour* was built at Macduff in 1929 as a typical Fifie, painted black with an external wooden rudder. She was a slightly lighter version of the *Charlotte Anne* TT49. In the early 1960s the boat was based at Scalpay, Harris, where she fished for lobsters that were often landed at Oban.

Forsyth Hamilton brought her to Tarbert in 1969 and registered her TT2. The original 44hp Kelvin engine was replaced by an 84hp Gardner. A Fifer trawl winch was also installed at this time.

During her early Tarbert days, Colin McBrayne of Campbeltown skippered her, before Arthur McFarlane bought the vessel in 1971. He fished her for a couple of years, mainly for prawns, queenies and scallops. According to Arthur, she was a very good sea boat.

After leaving the village, she was converted for pleasure use on the upper Clyde. A few years later, the *Endeavour* was seen line fishing for conger eels off the Isle of Cumbrae. Her conversion had not been too dramatic and she was easily recognisable.

TT4   TUDOR ROSE

52.4 O/L
49.2 x 16.5 x 6.1   **22.28 tons**

The *Tudor Rose* was built in 1949 by James N Miller and Sons Ltd of St Monance - a typical example of their herring ringers , having a rounded cruiser stern, powerful bow and familiar scrollwork carved into her name boards.

She was originally registered KY143 and, as the photograph shows, sported her brailer on the starboard side, in common with other East Coast ringers. The *Tudor Rose* later went to the Ayrshire coast registered BA180, and to Tarbert in 1968 from Mallaig, when Archie McKinnon bought her. He worked the vessel from Ardrishaig, up Loch Fyne, and also fished with lines around Lochboisdale, South Uist. Driven by an 112hp Kelvin engine, she never used the ring-net as a TT boat, but trawled mainly for prawns. The *Tudor Rose* pair-trawled with the Campbeltown registered *Girl Margaret* CN 158 (former *Stella Maris*) at the 1972 Loch Caolisport sprat fishery. She left the Tarbert fleet in 1974, and was later registered OB220 as the *Golden Sunset*.

***Tudor Rose* in her original condition as KY143.**
(Malcolm Stockdale Collection)

Tudor Rose lying at Oban as Golden Sunset OB220.
(John Crawford Collection)

Originally, BA127 registered and ring-net neighbour to the *Silver Spray* BA52, though some sources quote her as BA481.When they both came to Tarbert the *Twin Sisters* was re-registered TT8.

38.3 x 14.3 x 6.9   **17.14 tons**

George Forbes of Peterhead built the *Our Lassie* in 1952 for S Strachan, a local skipper. She was originally registered PD199, before being bought by Iain McNab in 1960 and re-registered TT8. When she first came to the village her crew members included skipper Iain McNab, John Black, Malcolm Smith, Douglas McNeil, Willie Smith and John McDougall (*Old Doods*).

Her wheelhouse was positioned well aft towards the stern with her mizzenmast in front of the wheelhouse. Iain McNab had the wheelhouse moved forward to the position in the photograph. She was painted green throughout her time in Tarbert and, unusually, had no mainmast as the mizzenmast and a 'wee crutch' or cradle at the bow supported the derrick. This is shown in the photograph, as is the unused tabernacle. The *Our Lassie* mainly used the seine-net for white fish and trawled for prawns, but did spend some time at the ring-net neighbouring various boats, when the masts were arranged in the usual cross formation. She partnered the *Nancy Glen* TT10 for about six weeks one year, the *Dalriada* TT77 for three seasons, and even the much larger *Maryeared* TT57 for a period of six weeks one summer. Peter McDougall recalls that she neighboured the *Maireared* TT135 for a year or two. When seine-netting she adopted the customary vertical mainmast and horizontal derrick arrangement. In 1969, she was sold to George Pattison of Arbroath, but still fished locally for a while. During this time her original wheelhouse was extended and she was painted light blue with a dark blue topstroke.

In 1979, the boat was sold to Peel, Isle of Man and registered PL92. Unfortunately, she was lost in a bizarre accident in 1992 when assisting the sinking boat *Don Bosco* PL12. The *Our Lassie* was hit by the *Don Bosco*, and also by another on-scene vessel, the *Acorn* PL2; she consequently sank. Thankfully, both casualty crews were taken aboard the *Acorn*.

The *Our Lassie* with fixed mainmast and derrick fishing in Inchmarnock Water.
(James McNab Collection)

Our Lassie **at the quay alongside the KingFisher.**
(Valentines Collection, St Andrews University)

46 x 14.5 x 6.4   **18.01 tons**

The first *Nancy Glen* was launched in August 1928 as the *Nil Desperandum* CN232 from the St Monance yard of J N Miller and Sons Ltd. Designed by Tom Miller, the boat was built for the hugely successful Campbeltown partnership of Robert (*Hoodie*) Robertson and John Short. Her wheelhouse arrangement was revolutionary in that it was positioned forward at the break in the deck. However, after five years, a replacement was installed in the traditional setting aft. The first boat to have her engine controls located inside the wheelhouse, the *Nil Desperandum* also had a Miller-designed winch that could be swivelled and used for discharging or working the net. She had a Kelvin 30hp engine, which was later superseded by a more powerful 44hp unit.

Her name was changed to the *Nancy Glen* in 1930, when she joined the Tarbert fleet under the ownership of Duncan McDougall, but skippered by his brother John. During the Second World War, she was requisitioned for service, and searched for submarines on navy patrols around Ireland and the Isle of Man. After the war, the *Nancy Glen* partnered the *Mary Bain* at the Isle of Man fishery. She was sold in 1949 and re- registered KY79, to be replaced by the *Charlotte Ann* TT49. Her buyer was Gavin Maxwell, who used the boat for shark fishing in the Minch. The names of the *Nancy Glen* and *Charlotte Ann* refer to the same lady, Charlotte Ann Glen, who was married to Duncan McDougall.

Nancy Glen **lying on the slip at Mallaig during the late 1940s and still TT registered.**
(John Crawford Collection)

39.9 0/L
37.6 x 15 x 6.3   **15.99 tons**

I was fortunate enough to be one of many Tarbert School pupils allowed out to watch the launch from Dickie's boatyard of the *Nancy Glen,* a dual-purpose boat built for Duncan and Archie McDougall. Nan McDougall named the vessel on January 14, 1960, in the company of Michael Noble, Secretary of State for Scotland.

The boat's length was less than 40 feet so that she could fish inside the three-mile limit. Driven by an 84hp Gardner engine the *Nancy Glen* had a distinct cruiser stern and a straight round-topped bow; she looked a pretty boat in her varnished finish.

In the late 1960s, Duncan retired, handing over to his sons, John, Robert and William, the youngest brother who joined in 1971. The boat was mainly used for prawn trawling but she did spend time ring-netting with the *Maisie* TT83 and the *Our Lassie* TT8. A fire on board resulted in repair work at Noble of Girvan. A new wheelhouse, constructed by Duncan McAlpine, was fitted which was larger than the original. The original engine was replaced in 1975 with a more powerful 150hp Volvo Penta. A later addition was a locally fabricated steel wheelhouse. In 1985, she was replaced by the *Nancy Glen II* TT100 and sold to Millport, Isle of Cumbrae. She retained her name for a while, but when the new owner's wife had a baby son, the boat was renamed *Boy Jamie* TT10. In the early 1990s, she was decommissioned at Cumbrae, beached and broken up by a JCB digger, when no bad wood was found in the boat - a credit to her builder of 30 years previously. This seems yet another waste of a perfectly good boat, which could be sailing today and giving pleasure or earning a living.

Nancy Glen **steaming into Tarbert on a snowy day in her original condition.**
(John Crawford Collection)

Nancy Glen **at Tarbert Quay rigged for ring-netting.**
(John Crawford Collection)

Nancy Glen **with replacement wheelhouse alongside the *Utopia* TT55.**
(John Crawford Collection*)***

39.9 x 13.3 x 4.7   11.22 tons

This boat was launched as the *Lassie* A93 at Macduff in 1931, and was a traditional 40-foot Fifie, painted black with an external rudder. Her name changed to the *White Rose* when she was sold to Arbroath and was re-registered AH20. Powered by a 44hp Kelvin engine, her Loch Fyne home base was Furnace, but she did visit Tarbert on many occasions. She fished mainly for scallops during the early 1960s, when her catch was usually discharged at Furnace and taken by British Road Services lorry to Glasgow for processing. In 1963, she was sold to Rothesay to be renamed the *Sheena Glen* RO49. At this time, she was painted green and looked a smart boat.

The *White Rose* at Crinan
(John Crawford collection)

22.5 keel
34.6 x 9.7 x 6.0   12.32 tons

John Fyfe, of Port Bannantyne built the *Sally* as a Loch Fyne skiff in 1902. She had the distinction of being the first Tarbert boat to be fitted with an engine. Her owner, John Johnson, decided to install a 7-9hp Kelvin in August 1908. She was later given an 8-10hp model. Despite being sold before 1925, I have included her because of this distinction. She left Tarbert in 1916 and re-registered BRD560.

Could this be the *Sally?* Identification is almost impossible due to tyres covering the registration at the starboard shoulder.
*(*John Crawford Collection)

49.4 x 15.8 x 5.8   **20.95 tons**

James Noble of Fraserburgh built the *Margaret Anne 11* in 1939, at the outbreak of the Second World War. Fitted with the popular 66hp Kelvin diesel engine, she was owned by the well-known Manson family of Mallaig, and originally registered OB49. When they ordered a new *Margaret Ann* OB79 in 1949, they sold the boat to her new Tarbert owners – George , Nicol and Alistair Bain. For a time, she partnered the *Mary Devereux* TT148 locally, and the *Frigate Bird* TT117 at the Isle of Man and Outer Hebrides fisheries. Her annual overhaul and repaint were carried out on the beach near McCallum's shed on Pier Road. The *Margaret Ann 11* was sold out of the village in 1954 to become KY56.

39.75 O/L
36.65 x 14.8 x 6.25   **15.26 tons**

The 35th boat to be built by Alexander Noble and Sons of Girvan was the *Caledonia* TT17. This 40-footer was launched for Peter Brown, Robert Ronald and John Johnstone of Tarbert on March 15, 1960, though her keel was laid in October 1959. Driven by a 66hp Kelvin engine, she was skippered by Peter Brown and fished from Tarbert for 20 years, firstly at the seine-net, but also for scallops and trawling out of the West Loch. The *Caledonia* ring-netted on occasions with the *Dalriada* TT77. Later in her Tarbert career she fell heir to a larger replacement wheelhouse, courtesy of the *Catherine Ann* TT31, when the latter was fitted with a new steel casing at St Monance. Originally, the *Caledonia* was similar to the *Dalriada,* but could be distinguished by a third rubbing strip along the side to afford the wooden hull more protection. She was also a fuller boat with higher gunwales than the *Dalriada.* As far as I recall, in her early days she was painted black with a varnished wheelhouse. Afterwards, she was painted blue with brown, then red topstroke.

The *Caledonia* was sold to the Isle of Man in 1980, and renamed *Threshlyn* PL98, thence to Kilkeel, where she was registered N98. In 1998, she was registered in County Donegal SO795, and was last heard of there in that year.

The *Caledonia* with the *Dalriada* and the *Maisie* berthed inside. Astern are the *Anne Marie,*
Nancy Glen, and the *Oak Lea* behind.
(Author's Collection)

*

Caledonia **coming into Tarbert harbour, rigged for ring-netting.**
(John Crawford Collection)

39.95 O/L
37.2 x 15.2 x 5.4   13.74 tons

Herd & MacKenzie built this boat in the 1950s as the *Green Pastures*, registered at Peterhead. Fitted with a 66hp Kelvin engine, she was a typical seine-net boat of under 40-feet. In 1969, she was re-registered TT18 and renamed the *Provider*. The boat was based in Ardrishaig, owned by George and Charlie McMillan, and Angus Johnson skippered her. She was used for catching prawns and remained in Ardrishaig until she was sold in 1975. The *Provider* was bought by the Ritchie brothers of Gourock and ceased fishing.

*

TT20 PRIDE OF THE CLYDE

53.4 O/L
49.7 x 17.5 x 6.5   **25.44 tons**

Pride of the Clyde **moored near the sailmakers awaiting sale in 1952. (John Crawford Collection)**

Walter Reekie of St Monance built this big, powerful boat in 1949; in fact, she was the last fishing boat to be built at this famous yard. At her launch, a piper in full highland dress played standing at her bow. Sadly, Mr Reekie fell between the *Pride of the Clyde* and the quay, sustaining serious injuries from which he later died.

Her Tarbert owner was Archie Kerr, who kept the vessel for just three years before selling her to Whitby. Reported to be a big vessel to work, she partnered the *Fionnaghal* TT65 for a while, as well as the *Maireared* TT113, and later the *Golden Gleam* TT30.

In 1952, M Leadley of Whitby purchased and renamed her *Success II* WY63. He later sold her to T H Turner of the same port, who, in turn, sold the boat down the coast to Scarborough as SH112. The *Success 11* became LH157 in 1960, but spent her last years in Bridlington, owned by Anthony Morris. A 6L3B 172hp Gardner engine powered her at that time. She was decommissioned in 1995.

*The Pride of the Clyde l*ater in
her career, as *Success II.* She
is seen here berthed at
Bridlington, East Yorkshire,
and painted dark green.
(Mike Wilson Collection)

46.0 x 14.0 x 6.5   **18.84 tons**

The first *Village Maid* TT21 was built by Wilson Noble of Fraserburgh in 1920. Her power was provided by a reliable 44hp Kelvin diesel engine. First registered as FR142, the boat came to Tarbert in 1925. Owned and skippered by Tom Jackson (*The Bear*), the *Village Maid* partnered the *Fiona*, a Loch Fyne skiff. Tom Jackson was the uncle of well-known Tarbert skippers, Willie and Neil Jackson. She was sold to Campbeltown in 1944 and was re-registered CN 35. The *Oak Lea* replaced her in 1947.

TT24 CATRIONA/ HARMONY

39.8 O/L
37.9 x 15.0 x 6.3   16.12 tons

This boat was originally the *Golden View* PD184, built in 1956 by Richard Irvin & Son Ltd, of Peterhead. Sold to Neil McAllister and renamed the *Catriona* in 1969, her new home port was Tarbert. Francis Lovie of Ardrishaig, who changed the name to Harmony, owned her latterly, fishing from Tarbert and Crinan. Powered by a 120hp Volvo Penta engine, the boat was sold in 1998 to Allan Morrison of Luing, Argyll, but retained Tarbert registry until 2000. During that year, the boat was taken off the fishing register and is still in Tarbert undergoing renovation. She has retained her original profile apart from a replacement steel wheelhouse that was fitted a number of years ago. The boat has now adopted her original name of *Golden View*.

***Harmony* in Tarbert Harbour with blue and black painted hull.**
(John Crawford Collection)

***Harmony* tied up at Tarbert quay undergoing renovation.**
(Author's Collection)

58.55 O'L
53.95 x 18.2 x 7.4   **32.7 tons**

This magnificent boat, arguably the finest ring-net model of her time, was another wonderful example from the Alexander Noble and Sons yard at Girvan, and a direct descendant of the first of her type, the 58-foot *Saffron* BA 182 – launched for the Ayrshire McCrindle family in 1951. The *Village Maid 11* was built for the Jackson brothers, Willie and Neil, and remained Tarbert registered until 1990.

Designers of later ringers, though excellent, tried to modernise the style on the drawing board, which did not really need to expand any further from an aesthetic point of view. The 20th century herring boats, of course, evolved from the innovative ideas of Campbeltown's Robert *Hoodie* Robertson, a man widely accepted as being the pioneer of advanced ring-net technology. He had started the ball rolling 38 years previously, when he had the first ever canoe-sterned ring-netter built.

The *Village Maid* was a big boat, but well proportioned with an attractive, yet modern wheelhouse. As the 38th boat completed by Noble, the keel was laid in October 1960, with the launch in May 1961. She was skippered by Innes Carmichael and Willie Jackson (*The Count*).

The *Oak Lea* TT131 was the vessel the Jacksons sold to make way for their new boat, which initially partnered the *Village Belle III* TT34 and later the *Village Belle IV* TT74, from the same builder in 1970.

The *Village Maid 11 was* the first Tarbert boat to carry an inflatable liferaft, which was stored on the wheelhouse roof. She also sported two white painted tyres as bow fenders, which was unusual in Tarbert boats. In the 1970s she had a new sloping roof type wheelhouse fitted at Carradale, though this alteration detracted somewhat from her appearance. The original engine was a 152hp Gardner 8L3B, but a more powerful 270hp Volvo Penta replaced this when herring catching in the Firth of Clyde became dependant on the pair-trawling method. She was sold in 1990 to Robert Summers of Mallaig, registered OB154, and sadly decommissioned in 1994. However, a museum in Mallaig is reported to have some of her equipment on display.

Above: *Village Maid II* alongside the *King Fisher* with the *Village Belle III* outside. (Author's Collection)

Right: *Village Maid II* at the quay. (John Crawford Collection)

54.1 O'L
50.3 x 16.2 x 63.0   **23.10 tons**

William Weatherhead and Sons of Cockenzie built the *Margarita* in 1948. She was a typical product of the yard, with a stepped deck and traditional wheelhouse. She transferred to Tarbert from Northern Ireland (B95) in 1961, when the McAlpine family bought the green painted vessel for £5000. As soon as she arrived, she was slipped at Dickie's boatyard, whereupon every inch of the hull was scraped and then varnished. Powered by an 114hp Gardner 6L3 engine, she ring-netted successfully with the *Maireared* TT135 and then *Maryeared* TT57 until the arrival of the new McAlpine vessel *Catherine Ann* TT31, when she was sold. She then fished from Birkenhead, registered LL7 until she unfortunately sank on September 3,1984.

This boat should not be confused with another *Margarita* TT141, which had been in the village in the late 1940s and early 1950s.

Margarita outside the *Maireared* at the quay.
(Author's Collection)

Neighbours at rest. The *Margarita* alongside the *Maryeared*, recently arrived in the village.
(John Crawford Collection)

TT27 PRIME

45.0 x 12.7 x 4.5 **11.57 tons**

The *Prime* was built in 1919 at Lossiemouth as INS123. In 1926, she was bought by Dugald McAlpine, grandfather of Douglas who gave me much assistance in the compilation of this book. She partnered the *Sweet Marie* TT106 and the *Maireared* TT135 during 1946 and 1947. Though not clearly visible on photographs, she was of clinker construction and had both sails and engine - a J4 44hp Kelvin petrol/paraffin - in her early days; originally she had no wheelhouse. After the Second World War, her old wooden rudder was replaced by a modern plate version at Dickie's boatyard. Robert Ross recalls that they used to curse her when listening for herring in the morning due to the noise created by wavelets slapping against her ridged clinker planking. He also remembers an incident when Dugald McAlpine lost his false teeth in the herring, but thankfully found them later when discharging at the quay. In another episode, he was working on the boat, which was moored over near Dickie's. Without warning, the *Prime* caught fire and, as there were no extinguishers on board, he had to act quickly or she would have been lost. He saved the day by crashing an oar through one of her planks, which resulted in a sinking, but it also put out the fire. She was refloated, repaired and continued to fish for many years. The addition of a wheelhouse transformed her appearance, and as the photograph shows it was positioned slightly to starboard to provide more room for working the ring-net.

The *Prime* was sold out of Tarbert in 1948, and records show she was lost at sea later that year.

The Prime at the quay with two of the crew sorting a catch of cod. Can you identify the other skiffs alongside and astern? The boat astern is possibly the *Seonaid*.
(Douglas McAlpine Collection)

TT27 FAIR DAWN

51.1 O/L
45.8 x 16.0 x 6.5 **21.43 tons**

John Stephen and Son of Banff built the *Fair Dawn* in 1947. She was previously registered FR298. The boat arrived in Tarbert in 1970, and remained in the fleet until 1986, when she was sold to Fleetwood. During her time in the village, she was painted blue with a traditional varnished wheelhouse. Owned by Innes Carmichael and skippered by Walter Scott, an AEC engine powered the *Fair Dawn*, which fished for prawns and herring. She had a traditional stepped wheelhouse, a feature uncommon in Tarbert boats.

The *Fair Dawn* was built in the same year and by the same yard as the *Fairhavens* TT140. These vessels were very similar in design, and the photograph depicts her in her original condition, registered BF136.

The *Fair Dawn* in her original form as BF136. (Malcolm Stockdale Collection)

*

34

The *Fair Dawn* as a Tarbert boat with blue hull and stepped wheelhouse. (John Crawford Collection)

TT30 BLOSSOM

40.5 keel
45.5 x 12.0 x 6.2   **15.23 tons**

There is confusion as to the exact date of this boat's launch, as records show 1909 and 1912. However, when new she was registered as a yacht at Aberdeen under the name of *Thelma*. She was then registered as a fishing boat A834. In 1918 she re-registered as ME209 and in 1920 she was renamed *River Mark* ME209. She then went west to Kyleakin, where the name changed to *Blossom* and registered BRD161. Alastair Parker, who helped with much of the information, explained the confusion over her year of build when he reported that some builders' records were later written from memory.

The boat joined the TT fleet in 1932; she kept her name but changed registration to TT30, and partnered the *Mary Munro* for a time She was an elliptical sterned, East Coast type powered by a noisy paraffin Atlantic engine, though she was later re-engined with a four cylinder, sleeve valve Kelvin that was unconventionally installed forward.

Eoghan McFarlane owned her, and the crew included John McFarlane and Calum McFarlane. John was the father of two well-known Tarbert residents, Jessie Bain and Mary McFarlane. They both relate the time that their father was fishing on the *Blossom* and a rope caught his leg and threw him overboard. He was saved thanks to the air trapped inside his big sea boots!

In the late 1930s the *Blossom* and the *Sweet Marie* were ring-net neighbours at the Firth of Forth fishery, based at Anstruther. On one occasion, local fishermen objected to the Tarbert men mending a tearing on the quay, and the work had to be carried out aboard the boats. The reason for the Fife men's unfriendly attitude is unclear.

The *Blossom* followed line fishing for a period line before being sold in 1942 to become PD313.

A rare shot of the *Blossom* on the shore at Dickie's boatyard. Despite the poor quality of the photograph, her distinctive stern is visible.
(Author's Collection)

54.7 O/L
50.5 x 17.6 x 6.8   **27.2 tons**

Possibly the finest fishing boat built by Dickie of Tarbert was the *Golden Gleam*. A magnificent vessel of perfect proportions, she slid into the waters of the harbour in 1949 for proud owner Willie McAffer; her varnished hull with darker stained topstroke made her live up to her name. Powered by a 120hp Gleniffer diesel, the *Golden Gleam* had a succession of neighbours, firstly the *Pride of the Clyde* TT20, the *Frigate Bird* TT117, and the *Ann Marie* TT150. Crew members who worked on her included George Dickson, John Johnson (*Blackie*), Calum McFarlane, Hughie McFarlane and Nicol Bain. On October 26, 1954, full to the hatches with herring, she ran aground on the north coast of Mull, on what is known today as *Gorrie's Reef*. Fortunately, all the crew survived due to the close proximity of the *Ann Marie* TT150, who picked them up, but sadly, the boat was a total loss. The *Evelyn* TT58, from Buckie, replaced her.

Just after her launch from Dickie's boatyard in 1949. Note the remains of the bottle at her bow.
(John Crawford Collection)

A very rare deck shot of the
***Golden Gleam.* Willie McAffer**
can be seen in the wheelhouse and
George Dickson is seen standing
on deck in the flat cap.
(Willie Dickson Collection)

39.9 x 14.0 x 6.5   **16.34 tons**

The *Girl Maureen* was another completion by the Alexander Noble and Sons yard at Girvan. She was boat number 10 when launched in October 1950 as BA128 for James Lamb of Duncan Street, Girvan. In 1970, she was bought by James Prentice and Peter Smith, and stayed in Tarbert for only two years. A 66hp Kelvin engine, typical of the Noble 40-footers, powered her. During her time in Tarbert, the *Girl Maureen* was painted green, and was similar in design to the *Dalriada* TT77, also built by Noble in 1954.

Douglas McAlpine recalls sailing on her for a week. They were fishing for prawns, towed for around one hour, and caught nothing. James Prentice then steamed to Lochranza, started fishing for queenies, and got 150 bags in one day!

58.2 O/L
52.2 x 17.9 x 5.7   **23.96 tons**

This boat, the fourth to be owned by the brothers Duncan and Archie McAlpine, was launched at the Dunbar yard of Weatherhead and Blackie in 1970. Named after Archie's daughter, she partnered the *Maryeared*, which was skippered by Duncan. Of larch on oak construction, the *Catherine Ann* cost about £35,000 to build. Her equipment included state of the art fish finding electronics as well as radar and two-way radiotelephones. Both ring-net and trawl winches were fitted, so she was a dual purpose vessel powered by a 230hp Gardner engine that burned more than eight gallons of fuel per hour. Her Norwegian-manufactured hydraulic steering was said to be fingertip light. The local newspaper *Argyllshire Advertiser* described the crew accommodation as being of very high order.

The *Catherine Ann* was a really attractive boat with a distinct sheer at the stern and varnished wooden wheelhouse of sloping-roof design, which was in vogue at the time. This wheelhouse was replaced a few years later at Millers of St Monance with a new steel casing similar to that of the *Maryeared* TT57.

Though the *Catherine Ann* was one of the last two operational ring-net boats in Tarbert she spent most of her time there pair-trawling for herring with the *Maryeared* and latterly single-boat trawling for prawns.

In 1996, the boat was sold to John Scott of Oban, before changing hands again three years later to Robert Summers and Mr Henderson of Mallaig. Unfortunately, she was decommissioned in 2002 and broken up.

Brand new in 1970, the *Catherine Ann* berthed at the quay.
(John Crawford Collection*)*

Dressed overall for the Seafood Festival with her new wheelhouse.
(Douglas McAlpine Collection)

TT32 SEONAID

39.5 x 12.0 x 7.5   16 tons

The British Marine Motor Co at Whiteinch on the Clyde built the *Seonaid*, Gaelic for *Janet*, in 1914. She was first registered at Broadford on Skye as BRD276. In 1932, her new owner, Archie McCaig, brought her to Tarbert. She ring-netted for herring during the Second World War, neighbouring Archie McDougall's *Flying Fish* TT37. Her construction was of a very high standard, and she was even registered A1 at Lloyds. Whilst fishing from Tarbert a 32hp engine powered her. She never had a wheelhouse; so fishing aboard her must have been very arduous in winter. In 1953, after a stay of more than 20 years, the *Seonaid* left Tarbert.

The *Seonaid*, nearest the camera, and featuring the *Polly Cook* TT85 and the bow of the *Sweet Marie* TT105.
(Author's Collection)

TT34 VILLAGE BELLE

49 x 14.8 x 7.2   23.50 tons

The first to carry this famous name was built by Walter Reekie of St Monance in 1932. She was ordered by the Jacksons of Tarbert, and successfully ring-netted with her neighbour the *Village Maid* TT21. On February 2, 1942, the Ministry of War Transport requisitioned her. She served her country well based at Freetown, Sierra Leone, until she was unfortunately lost in the Mediterranean Sea, near Alexandria, Egypt, towards the end of the Second World War.

TT34/TT66 VILLAGE BELLE III

54.5 O/L
49.8 x 17.5 x 6.3   24.71 tons

This was one of my favourite boats; as a teenager in the 1960s I had the good fortune of being allowed out on her by skipper Neil Jackson on several occasions. What a pity that video cameras had not then been invented! I recall Dougie Bain trying to explain the phosphorescence and feeling the wire, despite being busy on deck. He always had time to talk, and I remember him fondly. James N Miller & Sons Ltd built her at St Monance in 1949 as the *Margaret Newton* CN184. The Jackson family bought her in 1957 to replace the *Village Belle 11*, when that vessel was sold to Carradale and became the *Maid of the Mist* CN120. Initially the third *Belle* partnered the *Oak Lea* TT131, then later the new *Village Maid 11* TT25.

She was actually brought from the harbour in Bowling, when she was covered overall in Admiralty grey paint. The first task back in Tarbert was to scrape it all off down to the bare wood, and then varnish her. Willie Dickson recalls being involved and states that it was an awful job!

She was a beautiful boat, resplendent in her varnish coating, and typical of the Miller models of the day, though in later years she was painted dark blue. She had a bell at the front of the wheelhouse and a circular direction finder. Her mizzenmast was a somewhat thin affair, made from tubular steel, rather than wood. A 132hp Kelvin engine provided sufficient power to afford her the distinction of being one of the fastest boats in the fleet.

Her career after being sold in 1970 is rather complicated, but I shall endeavour to explain the sequence. She became CN44, based at Carradale, and during her time there was fitted with a larger, more modern, wooden wheelhouse by local joiner Neil (*Donna*) McDougall. She was then bought by former Tarbert resident Paul Gallagher and re-registered TT66. She worked from Tobermory as a scallop dredger for the next eight years until her sale to Kirkcudbright. Powered now by a 240hp Caterpillar engine, her new owner was Alistair Grant, who fished her until 1994, when she was decommissioned and sadly broken up. I contacted Mr Grant in that year to ask about taking some photographs, but unfortunately the *Village Belle* had been destroyed the previous month.

Left: The *Village Belle 111* in her original Tarbert condition.
(Author's Collection)

Below: Coming in to discharge with her hull painted blue.
(John Crawford collection)

**The *Village Belle III* seen here at West Loch Tarbert registered CN44, with her new wheelhouse.
(John Crawford Collection)**

49.5 x 14.8 x 7.2   23.74 tons

Walter Reekie of St. Monance built the *Mary Bain* for Archie McMillan of Tarbert in 1932. She was a few inches less than 50 feet in length and powered by a 66hp Kelvin diesel engine. The early photograph shows her with no mizzenmast and her brailer pole in the vertical position, which was how early ring-net boats configured their masts. She partnered the *Sheila* TT70 and the *Nancy Glen* (1) TT10. Originally, she was varnished but before leaving Tarbert in 1959 was painted bright green, and that is the condition I remember her in. She was sold to Tarbert, Harris and I believe she ring-netted from there as SY200. Because she was a Tarbert boat for 27 years, she often featured in postcard shots of the harbour.

An early photograph of the *Mary Bain* with vertical brailer pole, heading out of the harbour with a full load of passengers!
(Eric Irving Collection)

39.7 x 12.6 x 6.9   14.79 tons

John Fyfe, of Ardmaleish, Port Banantyne, built the *Osprey* in 1913, the same yard that launched the *Flying Fish* TT37. She was originally based at Dunure, registered BA143 before going to CN registry. She became a Tarbert boat in 1934, registered TT36, and owned by John Weir. Her fishing neighbours were, at different times, the *Little Flower* TT134 and the *Silver Spray* TT77. In 1958, she was sold to the upper Clyde and her Tarbert registry closed. There is some confusion about her new home port, but I have been told it was either Greenock or Port Glasgow, and that she was no longer used for fishing.

TT36 PIONEER

32.6 x 12.0 x 6.0   10.56 tons

The *Pioneer* was almost 40-years old when she took up Tarbert registry in 1971, though she was actually based at Rothesay. William Weatherhead & Sons of Cockenzie built her in 1932. Jock McArthur and Ronnie Gilbert owned and fished her for scallops until she was sold in 1983. Whilst sailing near Newport, Gwent she sank after running aground and was declared a total wreck.

The Pioneer **on the slip for a repaint. (Author's Collection)**

TT37 FLYING FISH

27.0 keel
37.0 x 11.0 x 5.5   10.07 tons

Another vessel from the Port Banantyne Yard of John Fyfe, the *Flying Fish* was built in 1907. Her power was provided by a 33hp Kelvin diesel engine, and was registered CN85 before arriving at Tarbert in 1932, when Archie Johnson and Archie McDougall bought her. She partnered the *Seonaid* TT32 for most of her time in the village. The crew never had the luxury of a wheelhouse, and she was the first boat that Robert Ross went fishing on. In 1947, the *Flying Fish* was sold to be used as a pleasure boat on the Thames.

Archie McDougall's grandsons, James and Kenny McNab own the current *Flying Fish* TT37.

Discharging at the quay with Duncan McDougall onboard, and John Johnson and Archie McDougall on the quayside. (James McNab Collection)

40.0 x 16.0 x 6.6   19.25 tons

She was constructed of steel at Eel Pie Island, Twickenham in 1968. Her power was provided by an 110hp 6LX Gardner, with Kort nozzle stern gear for greater towing capacity and easier steering ability. The *Girl Seona* was painted dark blue with a light blue band at the top. Iain McNab paid £17,500 for her, but also had a quote for a similar vessel made of wood. However, this would have cost £20,000, so the decision was made to break from tradition and go for the cheaper steel boat. The boat was sold in 1983, and replaced by the *Peaceful Waters* CN237.

Since that year, she has changed ownership, names and registrations several times. She became the *Fidelity* TT32, before going on to Troon under the name of *Red Baron* TN3, thereafter to Clachan as *Sincerity* TT259, and most recently to Gourock as *Lady Isle* TT263. Apparently, before she went to Gourock she had a mishap but was fully repaired by her latest owners.

Girl Seona passing the East Pier at Tarbert.
(James McNab Collection)

30.0 keel
40.8 x 11.8 x 7.0   15.17 tons

John Fyfe of Port Banantyne built the unusually named *Nellies* in 1920. She was ordered by Campbeltown owners and was registered CN165, later CN61. She arrived in Tarbert in 1933, when her registration became TT40. In March 1940, the records show that she was reduced in length to 40.4 feet and her weight to 15.02 tons. I am unsure why this minor alteration took place. She remained in the village until 1947. The *Nellies* was unfortunately wrecked off Islay on September 15, 1948.

A drawing of the *Nellies* TT40 heading out to sea.
(Illustration by Graham Ward)

39.8 O/L
37.2 x 14.9 x 6.8   16.96 tons

The *Destiny* was another boat completed by Dickie of Tarbert in June 1963, and Douglas McAlpine recalls having time off school to watch the launch; her keel had been laid at the end of January. She was built for Ronnie Johnson and Eoghan Smith. Powered by a Gardner 6LX 110 hp engine, she was a dual-purpose boat of just less than 40 feet, and mainly fished as a trawler, but also ring-netted at certain times. The *Destiny* partnered the *Nancy Glen* TT10, and the *Dalriada* TT77 for one or two years. Jimmy McFarlane (*Jap*) later worked her for a spell. She was a very smart and well-proportioned varnished boat with a distinct cruiser stern, which from some angles looks almost transom. She was sold in 1985 and registered LH421, but is currently based at Maryport, Cumbria, fitted with a larger replacement wheelhouse and a black hull, but still looks in good condition.

Ronnie Johnson produced an excellent book on the story of the Tarbert fishermen, which outlines the history of fishing from the village.

The varnished *Destiny* steaming into Tarbert in 1968.
(John Crawford Collection)

50.9 O/L
47.8 x 15.0 x 6.8   21.94 tons

The *Harmony* was built in 1946 by James Noble of Fraserburgh as INS4, later sold to become SY212, and then to Ireland in 1949; she was later converted into a yacht. In 1963 the boat joined the Tarbert registry numbered TT46, but should not be confused with the smaller *Harmony* TT24.

46.3 x 14.1 x 6.0   17.70 tons

The *May* was one of Weatherhead & Sons of Cockenzie's early canoe-sterned ring-net boats. She was built in 1929, registered BF328, and powered by a 44hp Kelvin engine. Willie McDougall brought her to Tarbert in 1956; Donald McNeil (*Peelins*) was a crew member. She fished at the ring-net for a year or two with the *Mary Bain* TT35, and was hired by Willie McAffer to partner the *Anne Marie* TT150 when the Evelyn TT58 had a new wheelhouse fitted at Dickie's boatyard. She changed hands when David McFarlane bought her from Duncan McDougall (*Dunky Mattha*). A fair amount of money was spent on the *May* in a refurbishment programme that included a new engine and modifications to the forecastle. The boat was sold in 1959 to become CN68, when Islay's Lachie Clark owned her. Here she creeled for lobsters, but was lost in 1968 off the north end of Islay.

A distant shot of the *May* as CN68 in Loch Melfort.
(John Crawford Collection)

39.9 x 13.6 x 4.7   11.48 tons

This boat was built by William & John Stephen of Macduff in 1932. She was named the *Golden Gleam* BF454, and sailed into Tarbert as such on April 15, 1954, being registered as the *Charlotte Ann* a few weeks later on May 8. The other *Golden Gleam* TT30 sank in October of the same year.

The *Charlotte Ann* was brought to the village to replace the first *Nancy Glen*. Of skaffie design with a wooden external rudder, she was, typically, painted black with a varnished wheelhouse. The *Charlotte Ann* fished using the seine-net under the command of Duncan McDougall. One of the members of her crew was Nicol Bain, who had survived the sinking of the *Golden Gleam* TT30. Her replacement was the new *Nancy Glen* TT10 in 1960, when the *Charlotte Ann* was sold to Caernarfon, and was seen there in 1961 still displaying her TT49 registration.

The *Charlotte Ann* TT49 undergoing a repaint. Nicol Bain is the crewmember in the middle. Can you name the other two? (Jessie Bain collection)

49.3 x 15.9 x 6.5   22.93 tons

The Sandhaven yard of J & G Forbes built the *Smiling Morn* for John Johnson of Tarbert. His daughter Margaret launched the £1,600 boat in 1933. This big, roomy sterned vessel was powered by a 55hp Atlantic engine, which soon gained a reputation for being rather unreliable. During her four-year stay in Tarbert, she partnered the *Isa Johnson* TT88, which was a much older and smaller boat.

In 1937 the *Smiling Morn* was sold to Wick and seine-netted from there registered WK70. She was acquired for war service in 1939 and, with a machine gun fitted at Aberdeen, patrolled from Wick and Scrabster. She even had the privilege of ferrying Winston Churchill at Scapa Flow. After the Second World War, a Gardner 5L3 replaced her original engine, and she was sold in turn to Tom Gunn of Wick, and later to Archie Reid of Stronsay, Orkney, where she was registered K827.

The latest chapter in the *Smiling Morn's* long life began in 1982, when David Merifield took her south to the Medway. When I was shown round her a couple of years ago in Gillingham Marina she looked immaculate, with her dark blue hull encircled by a gold line. Kept in excellent condition, she is now used purely for pleasure. At 70-years-old, the *Smiling Morn* is a credit to her designer and builders, and it is a pity that so many younger vessels have been broken up.

A drawing of the *Smiling Morn* TT50.
(Illustration by Graham Ward)

39.8 x 13.2 x 5.7   13.48 tons

W & J Stephen of Banff built the Mary Pat in 1931, originally as the *Catherine Margaret* BF310. In 1949 she was registered GK14, based at Greenock. She left Tarbert registry in 1966 and moved to Grimsby.

**The *Mary Pat* berthed at Crinan.
She was painted blue with brown
at the top.
(John Crawford Collection)**

48.4 x 15.6 x 6.6   22.42 tons

The *King Fisher* CN263 was built for Robert (*Hoodie*) Robertson of Campbeltown in 1933. Powered by a 66hp Kelvin, she had a distinct Walter Reekie of St Monance profile, with a round-topped stemhead and shallow forefoot cut away to facilitate good manoeuvrability. Eoghan McFarlane bought the *King Fisher* in 1950, and as TT55 she successfully ring-netted with the *Maireared* TT135, and later the *Silver Crest* TT75. From 1964 to 1966, the boat did not ring-net, but instead dredged for scallops. In the early 1960s, the vessel fell heir to the *Ann Marie's* wheelhouse, and this was fitted at Dickie's boatyard. The 'new' wheelhouse smartened up her profile, as the original was beginning to show signs of age. The photograph at Donaghadee shows her in her later condition. As a Tarbert ring-netter, she was easily recognisable by her brailer pole, which was always carried at a steep angle compared to other boats in the harbour. For several years, her topstrokes were painted brown, rather than varnished.

James McNab and David Goudie, both aged about 11, were going out on her one night, when the skipper asked them to run back to the Ca'dora café for some cigarettes. She was tied up outside the *Ranger* TT73, and when attempting to jump back aboard the *King Fisher* James misjudged his leap and plunged into the water between the two boats. That was the end of his night out at the fishing and he went home dejected to get dry! However, it certainly did not dampen his enthusiasm to become a fisherman.

After having been idle and tied up at the quay for a while, the boat was sold in 1966 to Donaghadee, and re-registered B604. Later she moved to Coleraine, where she bore the registration CE7. In 1984, she was seen on the River Bann, near Coleraine, in poor condition.

**The *King Fisher*
moored in the harbour
near Dickie's boatyard.
(Author's Collection)**

**On the beach for a repaint and varnish, with her 'new' wheelhouse.
(John Crawford Collection)**

The *King Fisher* after her sale to Donaghadee. She has the *Ann Marie's* old wheelhouse... A Weatherhead's top and a Reekie's bottom.
(Author's Collection)

54.0 O/L
52.05 x 17.65 x 5.9   24.39 tons

Another boat to bear TT55 registration was the *Utopia*. George Forbes & Co, of Peterhead, built her in 1948 as INS239. The move south to Tarbert came in 1972, where she remained until 1985. During this period, she had her wooden stepped wheelhouse replaced with a steel version at Dickie's boatyard. The *Utopia's* 132hp Kelvin was changed to a 220 hp Volvo Penta, which enabled her to pair-trawl with the *Taeping* TT79 for hake, and later at the herring with the *Brilliant Star* SH117. Her skipper was John McDougall (*Doods*). The boat was sold to Ireland and her new owner was Michael Sheehy of Dingle, County Kerry. Her latest registration of T43 closed in 2002.

Utopia **approaching Tarbert quay with her new wheelhouse, and her bow hawse pipes clearly visible. (John Crawford Collection)**

56.3 O/L
52.4 x 17.8 x 5.9 24.76 tons

Duncan McAlpine (*Moora*) had the *Maryeared* built in 1964 by Weatherhead & Blackie of Port Seton. This magnificent larch on oak varnished vessel was powered by a 200 hp Gardner 8L3B engine, later upgraded to 230hp. She has a 42-inch propeller, a fuel capacity of 780 gallons, and her steering was hydraulic. She cost

£18,000 new, which was a reasonable price considering that the *Catherine Ann* TT31, built only five years later, cost almost twice as much for a similar sized boat. She ring-netted with the *Margarita* TT26 and then later with the *Catherine Ann* TT31. In fact, they were the last pair of ring-net boats to work out of Tarbert. Her original wooden wheelhouse was replaced by one of modern design at Millers of St Monance; two years later, the *Catherine Ann* had a similar modification. Repairs to her planking came because of a scrape by the *Village Belle 111*'s anchor stock, and fortunately nobody was hurt.

In 1994, after 30 years service, the boat was sold to Eyemouth. Her varnish long gone, she was by then painted dark blue.

Around 2000 the *Maryeared* was sold out of fishing by A&P Johnstone to Nigel Musgrave, and thankfully not broken up. She is now used for diving work out of the Welsh port of Conwy. Much time and money has been spent on her conversion and in June 2003 she was advertised for sale on her own web site, something never even considered nearly 40 years ago when she was built! Many of her features were itemised in the advertisement and included seven original bunks, galley and two double bedded cabins in the former fish hold. She also has gas and diesel heating systems below decks and safety rails around the gunwhales. Wheelhouse equipment includes Racal Decca BT 360 radar, VHF radio and GPS systems. Therefore, this superb ring-netter continues to earn a living, but it is a pity that her partner, the *Catherine Anne* TT31, and most other boats were simply broken up or euphemistically decommissioned.

***Maryeared* on the stocks at Port Seton 1964.**
(Douglas McAlpine Collection)

The *Maryeared* tied up between the *Margarita* on the outside and the *Ann Marie*, painted blue on
the inside.
(John Crawford Collection)

A good stern and wheelhouse view of the *Maryeared*, with the *Margarita* and *Shemaron* CN244
beyond.
(Author's Collection)

***Maryeared* at Tarbert quay with her replacement wheelhouse.
(John Crawford Collection)**

53.1 x 16.1 x 6.2 24.85 tons

James Noble & Sons, Fraserburgh built the *Evelyn* as the *Afton Waters* BCK97 in 1946. Her first owners were the Murray family of Buckie. Following some form of disagreement, she was renamed the *Evelyn*, called for a daughter of one of the Murray brothers. She was easily recognisable as a Noble boat with her almost straight stern and round-topped stem. Her typically-designed narrow wheelhouse was locally known as a coffin! When new she was powered by an 88hp Kelvin engine.

Willie McAffer bought the boat in 1955 to replace the *Golden Gleam* TT30, which had been lost. When she arrived in Tarbert, she was, unusually, painted dark green as at that time almost all ring-net boats were varnished. However, she was later scraped and given a smart varnish coating. In later years, she reverted to green and two years before she left Tarbert she was painted blue.

In 1961, the *Evelyn's* Kelvin was replaced at Dickies with an 110hp Gardner 6LX, a power unit that soon became a popular choice of engine with other skippers. Her fuel tanks had a capacity of 150 gallons on each side. Whilst ring-netting, she burned about 80 gallons of fuel a week, but as a trawler this consumption dramatically increased to more than 240 gallons a week. She was also later fitted with a new wheelhouse at Dickies, similar to those of the *Oak Lea* TT131 and *Anne Marie* TT150

The boat's hold was capable of carrying 162 crans /650 baskets of herring, and on occasions was near to that limit.

When Willie McAffer retired, his nephew, Willie Dickson, took over the *Evelyn*. He skippered the boat for 20 years, ring-netting with her neighbour the *Ann Marie* TT150 for many years until the demise of that method of fishing. The *Evelyn* then spent several years prawn trawling until 1985.

She was decommissioned in 1985, and sold to Belfast for conversion. From there she moved to the Burtonport, Aran Island area and then on to Connemara, western Ireland. On a trip to Eire a few years ago, Willie Dickson tried to locate the *Evelyn*, but unfortunately, he had to return home before he could confirm her position or status.

In her original condition, as BCK97, unloading with the *Enterprise* at Ullapool. Note her name on the wheelhouse and the mizzen sail.
(John Crawford Collection)

Evelyn **coming into Tarbert, passing the Point. Note the snow on the hills at the other side of the loch.**
(John Crawford Collection)

The *Evelyn* on the beach later in her career. In this shot she is painted green, similar to her appearance when she first came to Tarbert.
(John Crawford Collection)

The *Catherine* was an old Loch Fyne skiff about which I could find little information. She apparently was neighbour to the *Peggy* TT334 during the Second World War when involved in ring-netting. She was owned at some time by Mattha Smith, and at another period by the Bain family. She never had a wheelhouse and was obviously very basic and typical of the pre-canoe-stern era. George Dickson crewed on her for a while, and she was similar in design to the *Seonaid* TT32. She was sold to Rothesay, where she unfortunately hit a buoy and sank in the bay.

49.8 x 15.0 x 7.0   23.53 tons

The *Fionnaghal* was another fine boat built by A M Dickie of Tarbert. She had a cut away forefoot, neat lines and a well-proportioned wheelhouse of classic design The boat was commissioned by the McDougall family, and served them well from her launch in 1937 until 1957. Robert Ross states that he and his school friends were given time off school to watch the launch. I find it heart warming that James Irving, the headmaster who was my grandfather, with a strict reputation, saw the launch of a fishing boat as being more important than Latin and Maths!

The *Fionnaghal* ring-netted with the *Maireared* TT113 (ex *Nulli Secundus* CN246), and was based near the family home at the Dubh-chaol-Linne, a small bay at the north east end of the harbour. She had two white tyres as bow fenders, an uncommon adornment in the Tarbert fleet. During the Second World War, she partnered the *Lily* of Campbeltown, when her skipper was Donald (*Tom*) McDougall.

When sold in 1957 she moved to Scarborough as a dogfish long liner, and became the *Marion* SH19. At this time, her sides were built up and rails were fitted. She was seen by Malcolm Stockdale of Grimsby in this condition and was described as being in a poor state.

The *Fionnaghal* was succeeded by the *Jessie McKinnon* CN196, later to be renamed *Fionnaghal 11* TT106.

The *Fionnaghal* moored at the Dubh-chaol-Linne with the crew sorting the nets. She had an appearance slightly similar to that of a Weatherhead ringer.

TT68 JUNE ROSE

The *June Rose* was an old Loch Fyne skiff and is remembered because she was painted a blue/grey colour. She did not have a wheelhouse and was usually moored over near the Doubh-choal-Linne. Dougald and David McFarlane of Larkfield, Garvel, Tarbert owned her. She was used mainly for scallop dredging during the 1960s.

TT70 SHEILA

31 keel
39.8 x 12.0 x 6.5   13.97 tons

John Thompson of Ardrossan built the *Sheila* in 1911. In her early years she was registered BA540. Later, she was a fairly typical converted Loch Fyne skiff with a wheelhouse. She spent three years ring-netting in the Tarbert fleet – from 1935 to 1938 – neighbouring the *Mary Bain* TT35, before being sold to Belfast.

The *Sheila* TT70 between the *Prime* TT27 and the *Flying Fish* TT37. Tied up ahead is the *Mary Bain* TT35.
(Author's Collection)

TT70 BOY KEN

51.7 O/L
47.4 x 17.5 x 6.4   23.89 tons

Coincidentally the *Boy Ken* TT70 was the 70th completion from the yard of Alexander Noble & Sons of Girvan. She was launched for James Prentice, Tarbert, and Associated Fisheries of Granton in March 1972, - another excellent example of the famed Noble craftsmanship. Driven by a 250 hp Caterpillar engine, she was typically built of larch planks on oak frames, and cost £48,000.

In October 1972, the *Boy Ken* featured in a *Sea Breezes* article about Aberystwyth harbour. Whilst fishing from there she used four dredges to catch scallops.

She carried a variety of gear and nets for scallops, prawns, sprats and herring, and had mixed success as a trawler. Unfortunately, due to the harsh economics of fishing at that time, she was sold to Tobermory in 1975 to become the *Frey* OB248. She was later sold to the Isle of Man, and is currently fishing as a scalloper from Castletown registered CT137. Recent photographs show her still varnished and retaining her original wheelhouse. The *Frey* looks in excellent condition and is a credit to her owner, William Caley of St. John's, Isle of Man.

Two 'boys' together. The *Boy Ken* TT70, in new condition tied up alongside the *Boy Lorne* TT94 at Tarbert quay.
(John Crawford Collection)

39.0 x 11.3 x 6.0   11.90 tons

Yet another Tarbert boat built by John Fyfe of Port Banantyne in 1917. She was originally built for Dunure owners as BA561. The *Mary Munro* had an external wooden rudder and a small wheelhouse. Her new owner, William McDougall, took her to the village in 1927, and partnered the *Maggie McDougall* TT2. In 1950, she was sold, like many other Tarbert boats, to Eire, where her new home port was Moville, County Donegal.

A drawing of the *Mary Munro* TT71.
(Illustration by Graham Ward)

55.3 x 17.9 x 7.0   31.81 tons

The *Golden West* was the first vessel to be completed by Fairlie Yacht Slip at the end of the Second World War. Launched in 1947, she was originally registered BA247, and based at Maidens. She joined the Tarbert fleet in 1965, having been bought by John McFarlane, son of the *King Fisher*'s skipper. The boat was powered by 6L3 114hp Gardner engine.

In 1955, she was reduced from 55 feet to 52 feet and underwent some conversion as a yacht before reverting back to a fishing boat. John Crawford, who kindly contributed many of the photographs in this book, worked on the *Golden West* for three months during 1967, when she fished for scallops out of Crinan.

She left Tarbert in1970, and two years later was re-registered BCK59. The boat later went to Eire, where she was registered in Sligo in 1993 as SO775. At this time, the vessel was powered by a 90hp engine, and owned by Peter McBride of Downings, Donegal. There is no fishing record of the *Golden West* after 1993. However, she and her sister ship, the *Golden Venture* BA274, are both to be found in the harbour at Dumbarton, having been converted for pleasure use.

John Crawford on deck as the *Golden West* sails into Crinan.
(John Crawford Collection)

TT68/TT73   CLAN MCTAVISH/ THE RANGER

40.5 x 12.5 x 5.3 12.07 tons

This vessel is unusual in that she was a Tarbert boat, registered in the village on two occasions under different names and registrations 17 years apart. In her first incarnation, she was the *Clan MacTavish*, based up the Loch at Ardrishaig. Launched by William Weatherhead & Sons of Cockenzie in 1927, the boat joined the Tarbert fleet new. She was built as a ring-netter and bore the typical Weatherhead profile of her 50-feet contemporaries. She remained at Ardrishaig until 1937, when she was sold to Ayrshire and renamed *The Ranger* BA206. In 1950, she returned to the Tarbert fleet, and this time was based in the village, numbered TT73.

When new she was six inches over 40 feet, but was later cut at the stern to just 40 feet – weighing in at just less than 12 tons. During her time in Tarbert she seine-netted for white fish, and also worked on the Crinan Canal when things were slack, assisting with repair work to the waterway.

Owned by Douglas McNeil, *The Ranger* was powered by a 44hp Kelvin engine, and was crewed by the other McNeil brothers - Donald and Laspey - and Angus Johnstone. The photograph shows her, or most of her, on the beach near Dickie's boatyard being overhauled and painted. She was sold to Grimsby in 1967 to become GY400, and her registry was cancelled in 1992.

The *Clan McTavish* on the beach at Ardrishaig. Note the wheelhouse is positioned far back at the stern.
(John Crawford Collection)

A close up of the *Ranger* after a repaint over at Dickie's boatyard.
(Author's Collection)

TT74 VILLAGE BELLE II

51.0 x 16.5 x 6.2 23.48 tons

William Weatherhead & Sons of Cockenzie launched the Jackson family's second *Village Belle* in 1940. She was the last boat to be completed there during the early stages of the Second World War, and had been an 'on spec' build. When the Admiralty commandeered the first *Village Belle* TT34, Willie Jackson heard about this new boat, went over to the East Coast and bought her from Weatherheads.

The records show that in July 1956 she was remeasured and listed as being five-and-a-half-feet shorter. During her Tarbert ring-net days, she partnered the *Village Maid* TT25 until 1944, followed by the *Oak Lea* TT131; Neil Jackson and Dougie Smith skippered her. She was sold to Carradale in 1957, when her name was changed to the *Maid of the Mist* CN120. The boat was a regular visitor to Tarbert afterwards, and often tied up alongside her successor, the *Village Belle 111* TT34.

On leaving Carradale, she went to Rothesay as RO56, where the hull was painted green. Later, she had her registration painted lower down between her two rubbing strips near the bow. She partnered the *Sunshine* CN76, and the *Silver Cloud* CN267 at the ring-net; Fred Brownie skippered both these Carradale boats. Tommy (*Tam*) Hughes, who had previously been part-owner of the little green ringer, *Pre Eminent* RO6, was in command of the *Maid of the Mist*. At the end of her ring-net fishing career, the mizzenmast was removed and a horizontal derrick rested in a steel A-frame support that was bolted to the deck a few feet forward of the wheelhouse.

Later in her career as the *Maid of the Mist* RO56.
(John Crawford Collection)

TT74 VILLAGE BELLE IV

59.9 O/L
55.9 x 19.1 x 8.3   39.88 tons

A few days after the arrival in Tarbert of the *Catherine Ann* TT31, a second brand new vessel steamed into the harbour. Owned by the Jackson family, this *Village Belle* was the fourth boat to bear the same name.

She was built by Alexander Noble & Sons of Girvan, and was their 65th launch on March 10, 1970. Powered by a 240hp Kelvin T8 engine, she cost in the region of £38,000. In addition to being a ring-net boat, the *Village Belle 1V* was also equipped for single/pair-trawling, and eventually rigged out for scallop dredging. At herring fishing she partnered the *Village Maid 11* TT25 skippered by Willie Jackson.

The latest electronic aids for fishing and navigation were fitted inside her typical Noble-designed sloping roofed, wooden wheelhouse. Conventional chain steering gave skipper Neil Jackson a feeling of greater response and control. Her masts were of a modern tubular steel design with a tripod at the bow. Below decks, the forecastle boasted a fitted galley and full size gas cooker.

The boat started life with a traditional varnished hull, but still looked resplendent painted in dark blue a few years later. The *Belle* has featured on many of the Ann Thomas Gallery products, ranging from tea towels to T-shirts.

She was sold, like the *Village Belle 111* TT34, to Paul Gallagher of Tobermory in 1989. Nine years later she was bought by John Baker, of Port Ellen, Islay, who kept her until 2002 before selling her to John MacAlister of Oban, from where she is currently fishing for scallops.

The varnish-hulled *Village Belle IV* coming into Oban.
(John Crawford Collection)

69

Looking magnificent in her blue painted hull at Tobermory.
(Paul Gallagher Collection)

48.0 x 15.0 x 6.4   20.74 tons

James Noble & Sons Ltd of Fraserburgh built the *Silver Crest* in 1934 as BA61. She was later sold to become CN76, before being bought by John McDougall (*Doods*) in 1950 and registered TT75. Investigation shows that when in Campbeltown as CN76 she partnered the *Lily Oak* CN131, skippered by George Ritchie. Her Tarbert ring-net neighbour was the *King Fisher* TT55. She also partnered the *Ann Marie* TT150 while the *Evelyn* TT58 was having a new engine installed. Unlike most other Tarbert boats, her red and green navigation lights were placed forward on the wheelhouse roof, rather than positioned at the back. A Gleniffer engine originally powered her, but a Gardner eventually replaced this.

Her TT registry was retained until 1986, though she had left Tarbert years before and was owned at Tighnabruaich, in the Kyles of Bute. I recall seeing her fishing for scallops off Arran on a still day in the mid 1970s. The *Silver Crest* was converted for private use and is apparently lying partly submerged at Fort Augustus on the Caledonian Canal.

The *Silver Crest* at Dickie's Yard during an overhaul. Beyond the *Anne Marie* donates her wheelhouse to the *King Fisher* berthed alongside.
(Photograph Dr Mayer. Author's Collection)

Silver Crest later in her career, in the Crinan Canal.
(John Crawford Collection).

37.0 x 13.0 x 3.0   9.11 tons

The *Bellemar* was built at Invergordon, Cromarty Firth in 1974 for Colin Mair of Tarbert, and Archie McGilp skippered her. Her original 84hp Gardner engine was replaced with a more powerful Volvo Penta. After this she had various owners, including Richard Johnstone, of Campbeltown; Glynn Arkell, of Carradale in 1998; Stephen Croll, of Carradale in 1999; and latterly Kenneth Brown, of Carradale in 2002. She was renamed the *Dalriada* at this time. The blue-painted *Bellemar* is constructed of wood with a transom stern and forward wheelhouse, and is based at Tarbert.

37.7 x 11.5 x 5.6   10.93 tons

John Thompson of Ardrossan built her in 1912 as BA52. The *Silver Spray* was a nabby and first registered in Maidens. At this time, she partnered the *Twin Sisters* BA127, fishing from the Ayrshire village. In 1927 both boats became Tarbert-owned and were skippered respectively by Donald (*Tom*) McDougall and Archie Kerr. The *Twin Sisters* was the original TT8, and partnered the *Little Flower* TT134 for a time. The *Silver Spray* – another boat Robert Ross recalls sailing on as a small boy in the 1930s – was sold to Oban in 1939.

39.9 O/L
34.7 x 14.6 x 6.6   14.3 tons

Robert Ross took delivery of the *Dalriada* from boat builder Alexander Noble & Sons Ltd of Girvan in 1954. She was the 20th boat built by this famous yard, which is still building and repairing boats today. Launched on December 3, 1954, she was powered by a 66hp Kelvin engine that was later upgraded to an 112hp R6 model of the same make to provide increased towing capabilities. From new, the *Dalriada* was painted black with a varnished wheelhouse, and had the famous Noble thistle emblem at her bow. She was a dual-purpose boat similar in design to other under 40-foot Noble boats, though mainly used for seine-netting. At ring-netting she partnered the *Caledonia* TT17, which was very similar to the *Dalriada*.
 She left Tarbert in 1978 and went to a number of different ports including:
Ardrishaig, Islay, Seahouses, Port Seton and Arbroath. She was later bought by Archie McArthur of Rothesay, who changed her name and registration to *Girl Margaret* 11 RO66. The boat then passed to Tarbert fisherman James McNab, who

was at this time based in Largs. Records show that in 1997-98 Raymond McKee of Kilkeel, County Down, owned her. In 2002, her registration changed to N912, when her new owner became Patrick Byrne of Ardglass.

The *Dalriada* rigged for ring-netting, steaming into Tarbert.
(John Crawford Collection)

The *Girl Margaret II* RO66 at full speed. Note the larger, replacement wheelhouse fitted by
Duncan McAlpine for Robert Ross.
(James McNab Collection)

TT78 BOY DAVID

39.8 O/L
36.5 x 15.3 x 6.2   15.58 tons

Herd & MacKenzie built the *Boy David* in 1959 as the *Strathdoon* BA122, based at Ayr. A typical 40-foot seine-net style of boat, she was brought to Loch Fyne in 1973 by Robert McDougall, and was used mainly for catching prawns. Originally, she was registered in Tarbert as the *Strathdoon* TT78, but changed her name in 1974. A 150hp Volvo engine was fitted during her Tarbert ownership period. She was sold a few years later to Colin Oman of Carradale, who retained the name and registration, and rigged the boat for scallop dredging. The *Boy David* was decommissioned in the 1990s.

The *Boy David* approaching Crinan.
(John Crawford Collection)

TT79 TRUSTFUL

40.0 x 14.6 x 6.5   15.77 tons

This boat was completed in 1932, another product of the Cockenzie yard of William Weatherhead & Sons. Originally built for East Coast owners at Fisherrow, registered LH110, she was fitted with a 66hp Kelvin engine. In 1947, she was sold up the coast to Stonehaven and registered A370.

The *Trustful* was bought by Archie (*Tar*) McDougall of Tarbert in 1966, but was only kept in the village for around a year. She spent some summer nights up Loch Fyne at Furnace. The boat returned to the East Coast in 1967, and changed her name to *Silver Fern*.

The *Trustful III* at Tarbert quay, with the *Our Lassie* berthed astern.
(John Crawford Collection)

54.0 x 19.0 x 6.0   24.88 tons

Forbes of Sandhaven built the *Catriona* in 1964 as the *Taeping* BA237 for the Andersons of Dunure, Ayrshire. Ronnie Johnson brought her to Tarbert, but the boat was later sold to former Tarbert skipper Neil McAllister, now of Ardrishaig. As the *Taeping*, she was a sturdy 152hp Gardner-driven ring-netter/prawner, and still has that heavier Forbes look. She is now powered by a 240hp Cummins engine, and is used as a trawler.

When she became *Taeping* TT79 in the early 1970s, the light green-hulled boat pair-trawled for both hake and herring with various neighbours. Today, Neil McAllister concentrates mainly on catching quality prawns. The *Catriona*, now painted dark blue, is photographed alongside another former ring-net boat, the *Prospector* TT25 at Tarbert harbour in 2002.

The *Catriona* berthed alongside another former ring-net boat, the *Prospector* TT25, which was built by Noble of Girvan. (Author's Collection)

35 Keel
45.3 x 13.0 x 5.6   15.36 g tons   14.98 tons

William Mahood of Portavogie built the *Willing Lad* in 1913. When new she was registered B513, but changed to Tarbert registration in 1928. A 66hp Kelvin engine provided the power. James McFarlane skippered her, and the crew included Angus and Calum McFarlane. The boat remained in Tarbert until 1940, when she was sold back to Northern Ireland and registered B513 for the second time. I have been told that during her time in the village she was varnished.

TT83 MAISIE

39.3 O/L
37.4 x 14.7 x 6.1   15.09 tons

The *Maisie* was yet another James Noble (Fraserburgh) Ltd boat, built in 1952 for Archie Kerr of Tarbert. He ordered her to replace the much bigger *Pride of the Clyde*. Powered by a 66hp Kelvin diesel engine, she arrived in Tarbert with a varnished hull, but only retained this finish for a couple of years before being painted black as shown in the photograph. A green canvas cover protected the lower part of her wheelhouse, to prevent damage to the wood from the muddy seine-net ropes. As well as white fishing she also ring-netted with the *Nancy Glen* TT10 in the early 1960s. Her crew included Iain McNab, who spent eight years on the boat before he bought the *Our Lassie* TT8. In 1964 she left Tarbert and sailed south to Caernarfon and was registered there as CO154.

The *Maisie* minus her masts after a repaint.
(Author's Collection)

TT85 POLLY COOK

46.0 x 13.1 x 5.5   18.58 tons

Weatherhead & Sons of Cockenzie built the *Polly Cook* in 1926. She was launched as the *Mary Sturgeon* BA40, a typical early canoe-sterned ring-netter with her small wheelhouse positioned well aft at the stern, and the lower rubbing strip finishing feet short of the bow and stern. Powered by an 88hp Kelvin K3 diesel engine, the *Mary Sturgeon* was, in 1933, the first ring-net boat to be fitted with a brailer and mast. Until then, the herring were taken aboard by a pole and basket, known as the *stick basket*, which was very heavy and time-consuming work. She was later sold to Carradale, registered CN255, and shortly afterwards her name changed to *Polly Cook*. At this time her wheelhouse was moved forward slightly to the more usual position.

She joined the Tarbert fleet in 1947, as did several other boats. However due to slack fishing, she left the village in the early 1950s, but retained her TT registration until 1961. During this time, she fished from Fleetwood.

When I was a small boy my uncle, Hugh Irving, who grew up in Tarbert, had a half model of the *Polly Cook* in his Edinburgh home. He told me that I could have the model when I grew up, but sadly that never materialised!

The *Polly Cook* tied up at the old quay clearly showing her Weatherhead profile of the early canoe-stern ring net boats. The *Seonaid* TT32 is moored alongside and the boat beyond is possibly the *Mary Devereux*.
(John Crawford Collection)

TT88 ISA JOHNSON

41.2 x 12.8 x 5.9   14 tons

Archibald Leitch built the *Isa Johnson* at the Battery yard, Pier Road, Tarbert in 1920. Fyfes had previously owned this yard, which today is used by Tarbert Sailing Club. She was built for John Johnson (*Big Johnny*) who also owned the *Isa MacGeachie*, originally from Campbeltown. Robert Ross recalls going out for a night's fishing on her as a wee boy! She had a wheelhouse and was powered by a Bolinder engine, which was later replaced by an Atlantic unit. For a while she ring-netted with the *Smiling Morn* TT50. She was normally moored across at the Dubh-chaol–Linne, though the photograph shows her beached near to where she was built. In 1940, she was sold for £44 to Belfast, and registered B145.

The *Isa Johnson* on the beach near the Battery. Alongside her is the *Smiling Morn* TT50, her ring-net partner.
(Author's Collection)

48.3 O/L
44.9 x 14.6 x 6.3   18.58 tons

Though registered as a Tarbert boat, the *Florentine* was based up Loch Fyne at Furnace, and moored at the Sand Hole near Minard. She was only in the fleet for a year, from 1967 to 1968. However, she was no stranger to Tarbert, and was often seen in the village, as the photograph shows. Built in 1932 by James Noble of Fraserburgh as CN197, the boat was succeeded in Carradale by another *Florentine* CN74 (ex-*Mallaig Mhor*), from the same builder. As CN197 she features on the front cover of this book, and ring-netted with the *Irma* CN45 for many years,

The *Florentine* left the CN fleet in 1959 to become W197; in 1965 to OB122; and SY27 before being registered TT92.

The boat featured in an article in the September 1932 edition of *The Motor Boat*. On her delivery voyage from Fraserburgh to the Forth and Clyde Canal at Grangemouth she covered the 142 nautical miles non-stop. It took her 17 hours, 19 minutes at an average speed of eight point two knots, and she burned 34 gallons of diesel oil. The fuel consumption was calculated at less than two gallons per hour, which was described as a remarkable performance.

Right: A weekend visitor to Tarbert, the *Florentine*, displaying her typical Noble profile.
(Author's Collection)

The *Florentine* TT92 at Furnace rigged for ring-netting. (John Crawford Collection).

39.9 O/L
38.0 x 14.5 x 5.8 14.38 tons.

Tommy Summers of Fraserburgh built this boat in 1950 as the *Gladiolus* BF225. She was afterwards sold to become FR173. The vessel was added to the Tarbert fleet in 1969 under the skipper-ownership of Willie (*Tar*) McDougall, and remained until 1974, when she was replaced by the *Braes of Garry* (renamed *Silver Fern 11*), which was skippered by John *Jockus* Johnson. On her sale to the East Coast, her name was changed to the *Galilean* FR136, before later becoming SY53 in 1985.

A few years ago, the boat was bought by a group who were going to send her to the West Indies to assist with the development of a revised fishing industry, following a major volcano tragedy. However, this plan never came to fruition and she was put up for sale, minus her fishing gear and wheelhouse.

The *Silver Fern* berthed at the quay, rigged for seine netting.
(John Crawford Collection)

46.3 x 14.7 x 6.8   20.83 tons

The *Jessie* was another Fraserburgh built boat, but this time in 1932 from the yard of Wilson Noble. She was originally registered INS228, but was on the Tarbert register four years later in 1936. Of Fifie type design with a prominent wooden rudder and powered by a 66hp Kelvin diesel engine, her skipper was Archie Kerr, who also skippered the *Pride of the Clyde* and later the *Maisie*. In fact, the *Pride of the Clyde* was built to replace the *Jessie*. Robert Ross remembers being tied up alongside the *Jessie* at Port Erin, Isle of Man, before setting off for Tarbert later that day.

In 1950, she was sold to the Dougall brothers of Rothesay and re-registered RO47, her name having already been changed to the *Guiding Star*. She was cut to 40-feet at Robertson's Sandbank yard, and then used as an inshore seine-netter. The vessel finished her fishing career as a scalloper working out of Port Ellen, Islay.

39.6 x 14.3 x 5.7   14.53 tons

Albert Palmer of Portavogie built this boat in 1949. During the early 1960s, she was called the *Breadwinner* BA92, based at Largs, when she was fitted with a 6LW Gardner 84hp engine. The boat was bought into Tarbert as the *Ebeneezer* FR282 in 1967, and remained in the village until 1976. Named after owner Archie (*Tar*) McDougall's son Lorne, and later skippered by his other son Ally, the boat was a seine-netter and prawner during her time in the village. In October 1976 the *Boy Lorne* was re-measured to 38.1feet, and reduced to 13.97 tons. She was sold to Donaghadee and re-registered B256.

Ally McDougall then bought the *Golden Dawn* from Carradale and renamed her *Boy Lorne 11* TT113. Though further information is outside this study, it is interesting to note that this Herd and McKenzie vessel returned to Tarbert in the late 1990s as the *Starlight*, and is now in the Eire port of Wicklow.

The *Boy Lorne* was seen in Howth, Ireland in 2002, rigged for trawling, and still bearing the same name.

**The seine-netter *Boy Lorne* painted blue and brown at Tarbert Quay. Astern are the *Silver Fern*
TT119 and the *Our Lassie TT8*.
(John Crawford Collection)**

49.3 x 16.5 x 6.7   24.53 tons

The *White Rose* was another boat built by James Noble of Fraserburgh in 1949. Similar to the *Evelyn*, but with a flush deck, she was registered in Peel, Isle of Man, as PL18 before coming to Tarbert in 1967. Her original Gleniffer engine was upgraded to an 110hp Gardner 6LX model.

The vessel's name was later changed to *Third Wish*, though this was never official.

The boat only fished out of Tarbert for two years, before being sold back to the Isle of Man in 1969, and re-registered as *New Venture* PL28.

52.3 x 17.0 x 6.4   23.26 tons
April 1957 to 49.8 x 17.0 x 6.4   24.38 tons

This typical Miller boat was built at St Monance in 1949. She was originally purchased by the Robertson family of Campbeltown and named the *Almanzora* CN54. She was bought in 1957 by the McDougalls of Tarbert to replace the *Maireared* TT113. She and the *Fionnaghal* TT106 were ring-net partners, and both boats moored over at the Dubh-chaol- Linne, close to where the crew lived. Note from the photograph that her winch was not the usual model favoured by most ring net-boats, but was similar to that of the *Golden Gleam* TT30.

In 1962, she was sold to Eriskay and renamed *Sancta Virgo* CY254. The boat ceased fishing in 1979 and was sold for use as a pleasure vessel.

**The *Mhairead* discharging at Ayr harbour. The *Fiona* CN165 and the *Maid of the Mist* CN120 are berthed astern.
(Eric Irving Collection)**

The *Mhairead* approaching
Tarbert quay in the late 1950s.
(Author's Collection)

TT105 SWEET MÁRIE

21.0 keel
35 x 10.1 x 6.0   9.54 tons

Thomas Fyfe at the Battery, Tarbert built the *Sweet Marie* in 1902. Records show that her first registration was 405AG. Later that year the Fishery Office in Ardrishaig moved to Tarbert, marking the beginning of the famous TT registration. Some AG-registered boats retained their registration until 1907.

Skippered by Archie McFarlane, she ring-netted with the *Prime* TT27 (*Skabie*) and was crewed by John Smith (*Hairie*), Dugald Smith (*Dugsack*) and Duggie Smith. Powered by 22hp Kelvin engine, the *Sweet Marie* never had a wheelhouse, and compared to other boats during the 1940s and 1950s was very basic. Her fishing registration ceased in 1956.

The *Sweet Marie* in painted condition,
moored near Dickie's boatyard in the
mid 1950s.
(Author's Collection)

TT106 SCARBH

39.9 x 13.4 x 6.2   14.92 tons

The *Scarbh* was built for Tarbert owners in 1947 by the Gourock yard of J Adam & Sons. She was just less than 40-feet long, and fished from Tarbert until 1951. She was then sold to Troon and converted for use as a pleasure vessel, still bearing her original name. She is currently owned by Nick Ryan, of the Crinan Hotel, where she is moored in the canal basin. As the photograph shows, the vessel is immaculately finished in varnish and retains her original wheelhouse. Every four years she is scraped back to the wood and revarnished at Crinan Boatyard.

The *Scarbh* tied up at Crinan.
(Author's Collection)

TT106 FIONNAGHAL

52.0 x 16.8 x 7.0   27.52 tons

William Weatherhead & Sons of Eyemouth built this attractive boat. She was unique in that all previous Weatherhead boats in Tarbert had come from their Cockenzie yard. The vessel was launched as the *Jessie McKinnon* CN196 for Neil McLean of Campbeltown. Power was provided by a 120hp McLaren diesel engine, but this was replaced with an 114hp Gardner by Peter McDougall in 1956, when the boat was sold into Tarbert.

She was bought to replace the original *Fionnaghal* TT65, and ring-netted with the newly acquired *Mhairead* TT104. Both boats were maintained in immaculate condition, and looked a fine, but contrasting pair moored at the Dubh-chaol-Linne. Later, after the sale of the *Mhairead* she ring-netted with the *Erica* BA73.

According to Peter McDougall, she damaged her keel after grounding on a rock near Lochboisdale Pier, South Uist. Apparently, most of the damage was done as she was being towed off the rock, causing it to twist slightly. The *Fionnaghal* could be easily distinguished by the exaggerated sheer at the stern, described as a "banana stern" by Peter McDougall. A similar style of stern was to be repeated later on the *Catherine Ann* TT31.

In 1967, this lovely boat was sold and re-registered LH456, based at Newhaven on the Firth of Forth. She was unfortunately wrecked in May 1974 on Insch Island (*Sheep Island*), north of Easdale.

**Right: The *Fionnaghal* moored at the Doubh-chaol-Linne.
(Author's Collection)**

**Below: On the beach for a repaint, with the *Our Lassie* TT8 tied up beyond.
(John Crawford Collection)**

The *Fionnaghal* after her sale from Tarbert, as LH456.
(John Crawford Collection)

46.6 x 12.0 x 5.9   14.92 tons

The *Titan* was built in 1944 at Granton on the Firth of Forth. She was under Tarbert ownership by 1953, and remained under TT registry until 1964. She was then sold and converted at Leith into a pleasure boat.

53.0 O/L
49.7 x 16.8 x 6.5   24.42 tons

James N Miller & Sons Ltd built the *Endeavour* 11 in 1948 as the *Boy Danny* CN142 for the Stewart family of Campbeltown. Similar in design to the *Mhairead* TT104 and the *Village Belle 111* TT34, she was a regular visitor to Tarbert as a Campbeltown boat; she also spent a season ring-netting with the *Dalriada* TT77. However she was unusual in that, though being owned from new on the West Coast, she had her forecastle hatch on the port rather than the customary starboard side, and her stovepipe was also on the opposite side – more in keeping with an East Coast boat. The *Boy Danny* was one of three Campbeltown ringers that suffered damage in the pre-radar days when they ran aground in dense fog on passage from Oban, after discharging very large catches of herring. The other two vessels involved were the

Moira CN33 and the *Mary McLean* CN193. The *Boy Danny's* keel was weakened as a result of the incident, and this was to prove detrimental to her later fishing career.

She arrived in Tarbert in 1977, under the command of Arthur McFarlane, who had previously skippered the *King Fisher* TT55 and the *White Rose* TT100. Though varnished when new, she was one of the first ring-net boats to be painted blue, and her wheelhouse was painted brown rather than varnished.

She was sold to Portavogie, Northern Ireland, in 1980, and registered B327. Records show that she was last registered as a fishing boat in 1995 and was broken up two years later.

The *Endeavour II* TT112 at the West Loch pier. (John Crawford Collection).

48.0 x 15.0 x 7.1   23 tons

The *Maireared* was built in 1932 by Walter Reekie, St Monance for Robert (*Hoodie*) Robertson of Campbeltown. Her original name was *Nulli Secundus* (second to none), and she was registered CN246. The boat was similar in appearance to the *King Fisher* TT55, built for Robertson by the same yard in 1933.

She was bought in 1938 by the McDougalls of Tarbert and re-registered TT113. Her ring-net partner was the *Fionnaghal* TT65 for almost all of her Tarbert career.

It is interesting to note that there was another *Maireared* TT135 in the village at the same time, but more about that boat later. There have been two other boats named *Margaret* in Gaelic in addition to the above, both with different spellings. I have been told that *Mhairead* is the correct version, but as my only contact with Gaelic was as an 11-year-old singing at the Argyll Mod for Tarbert School, I cannot confirm this!

In 1957, she was sold to Ireland and renamed the *Irish Rose*. The *Mhairead* TT104, ex-*Almanzora* CN54, succeeded her.

Unconfirmed reports suggest that years later she sank off Majorca in the Mediterranean, as the result of an exploding gas cylinder on board.

On a visit to the North, the *Maireared* TT113 is seen here unloading at Mallaig. Nearest the camera is the *Stormdrift* BA364.
(Valentines, University of St Andrews Collection)

89

SUNBEAM

52.0 O/L
47.1 x 16.4 x 6.5   22.59 tons

James Noble of Fraserburgh built the Sunbeam BCK165 for Willie Reid in 1947. She was used as a ring-net boat based in Portgordon, and neighboured the *Afton Waters* BCK97, which later became the *Evelyn* TT58. This partnership lasted while the *Concord* was being built, which then became the regular neighbour of the *Afton Waters*.

In 1974, Robert Ross brought her to Tarbert, though he also still owned the *Dalriada* TT77. When she arrived in the village she was painted green, but this was later changed to blue. She was decommissioned in 1995 and, despite attempts to have her preserved in conjunction with the Heritage Centre, the *Sunbeam* was broken up at Campbeltown.

The *Sunbeam* TT117 at the quay with the *Caledonia* TT17.
(Author's Collection)

FRIGATE BIRD

50.3 x 15.0 x 5.8   19.69 tons

Built in 1922 by James N Miller & Sons Ltd of St Monance, this was a fishing boat design that was to remain basically unaltered for the next 50 years. The *Falcon* CN97 and the *Frigate Bird* CN99 were the herring industry's first canoe-sterned ringers, and were ordered by Campbeltown's Robert (*Hoodie*) Robertson – a man widely regarded as being Scotland's most innovative ring-net fisherman of the time. W G McBride, who based his novel plans on Norwegian fishing boats, designed her. She was powered by a petrol/paraffin Gleniffer 18/22hp engine. A new feature, in addition to the canoe stern and the cut away forefoot, was that she was decked from stem to stern. She was very manoeuvrable, and this advantage made her successful as a ring-netter. The *Frigate Bird* was later re-engined with a with 66hp Kelvin diesel.

Duncan McDougall took her to Tarbert in 1947. For a while, she neighboured the *Golden Gleam* TT30, but also was the ring-net partner of the *Fairhavens* TT140. The boat was photographed in Whitby, but is hardly distinguishable in a packed harbour. She was sold to Stornoway in 1955 and became SY41.

Duncan's nephews, Kenny and James McNab, own the current *Frigate Bird* TT117.

56.0 O/L
53.5 x 17.3 x 7.4   30.82 tons

The *Silver Fern* is possibly just outside the scope of this book, but I have included her because she was built as a ring-net boat. She was launched at Fairlie in 1950; having been built by the Fairlie Yacht Slip Ltd. Originally owned by Andy McCrindle as BA101, she was later registered as CN261 and then BA162. She only fished from Tarbert for a year (from 1978 – 1979) under the ownership of *Irish Tommy*. From Tarbert she went to Helston, Cornwall, where William Tate owned her and changed the name to *Silver Fern of Newlyn* PZ119. At this time the vessel was powered by a 172hp Gardner engine. The boat later moved north, and in the late 1990s was owned by NC Trawlers of Blackpool, where she was decommissioned in 2001.

The *Silver Fern* before she became registered as a Tarbert boat alongside the *Maid of the Mist*, which had previously been registered in Tarbert. (John Crawford)

TT131 OAK LEA

50.9 x 16.1 x 6.5 20.96 tons

The *Oak Lea* was one of several Tarbert boats built by James Noble of Fraserburgh. She was launched in 1936, and registered BCK51. However, when Willie Jackson purchased and re-registered the vessel TT131 in 1947, her name was not changed to *Village Maid* as may have been expected. The *Oak Lea* partnered the other Jackson boat, *Village Belle 11* TT74 until 1957, when the latter was sold to make way for the *Village Belle 111* TT34. This partnership lasted until 1961, when the *Oak Lea* was sold and replaced by the brand new *Village Maid 11* TT25.

When she left Tarbert in 1961, she went to Tobermory, and then Oban as OB74. Her registry was cancelled in 1986 at Kyleakin, where she was beached and left to the elements. She was later placed on a low-loader, taken to the mainland, and can be seen today in poor condition lying against the outer wall of a farm steading at Kirkton, near Kyle of Lochalsh.

She was an attractive boat; the photograph shows her just before she left Tarbert, apparently sporting a recent coat of varnish and silver paint. Her replacement wheelhouse, by Dickies, is clearly visible, as is her slender mizzenmast and unusual square direction finder. On the beach, behind her is the *Village Belle 111* TT34, still undergoing painting and varnishing.

A rare shot of the *Oak Lea* TT131 after a repaint. Her neighbour, the *Village Belle III* is still on the beach behind her.
(James McNab Collection*)*

The *Oak Lea* as OB74 berthed at Kyleakin. She is painted black but retains her Dickie's wheelhouse.
(John Crawford Collection)

45.8 x 14.2 x 5.6   16.39 tons

The *Monsoon* was another vessel from James Noble of Fraserburgh. She was launched as BA265 in 1933, and joined the Tarbert fleet in 1948; she remained in the village until 1953. The *Monsoon* was a smaller version of the *Oak Lea* TT131, and ring-netted with the *Margarita* TT141 (ex-BA56). An 80hp Gleniffer engine provided power. She was not actually owned in Tarbert, but was skippered by Malcolm Smith. As well as ring-netting for herring, she also spent some time fishing for scallops. During her ring-net days, she wandered far away to places including Wick, Montrose and Whitby. According to my contributors, she is remembered for the prolific emission of exhaust smoke. After the *Monsoon* left Tarbert in 1953 she was converted for use as a cargo boat, based at Craignure, Isle of Mull.

31.0 keel
43.0 x 12.5 x 6.5   15.72 tons

Robert Wylie of Campbeltown built the *Little Flower* in 1913. Her first owner was John McKay, and she could best be described as a big Loch Fyne skiff. According to Robert Ross, who sailed on her, she had a "cod's head and a mackerel's tail:" in other words big broad shoulders and tapered to a narrow stern. She was bought into to Tarbert in 1943 and sometimes fished for sprats by dropping anchor and lowering a beam over the stern. The crew then went to their bunks for a few hours, while the fish came in on the tide and into the nets. The men arose and lifted the beam and net full of fish. On December 3, 1944, exactly 10 years before the launch of the *Dalriada* TT77, she collided with the *Enterprise* CN256 and sank inside Otter Spit.

48.0 x 13.9 x 6.1 18.31 tons

William Weatherhead of Cockenzie built the 'wee' *Maireared* in 1932 as BA196. She arrived Tarbert in 1948, and remained there for 17 years. Robert Ross accompanied Archie McAlpine to buy her from Fairlie and bring her back to Tarbert. The *Maireared* ring-netted with the *King Fisher* TT55, and later with the *Margarita* TT26. Throughout her Tarbert career, she retained a varnished hull and original wheelhouse, which had two narrow, horizontal windows at the back. Its door was set into the starboard side panelling, unlike the after end as on most other ring-net boats. Douglas McAlpine relates that she was re-varnished and done up to sell, but whilst tied up at the present fish farm boat jetty an old MFV nearing the quay hit her, causing the deck to split. Fortunately, she was repaired, and eventually sold to the Thames in 1965 for use as a pleasure boat.

Above: The bow of the *King Fisher*, at her usual berth , with the *Margarita* TT26 and the *Maireared* alongside. (Fred Sykes Photograph. Author's Collection)
Below: The crew of the *Maireared* from left to right; Duncan McAlpine, Donald Johnson, Archie McPherson, John Johnson and Dugald McAlpine. (Douglas McAlpine Collection)

TT138 CLAN MCNAB

42.8 x 12.0 x 7.5   17.33 tons

David Munro, of Blairmore, built the Clan McNab on Loch Long in 1922. Robbie McNab bought her in 1923, and based her at Minard, upper Loch Fyne. The boat was a traditional Loch Fyne skiff with a length of slightly more than 40-feet. She ring-netted with the *Sireadh* TT150 for five years, and was sold in 1928, but there is no record of her after that. It is understood that she was broken up at an age of only six years!

TT140 FAIRHAVENS

51.0 O/L
46.3 x 16.0 x 6.5   21.67 tons

John Stephen & Son of Banff built the *Fairhavens* in 1947. She was a typical product of the yard, being rather sturdy in appearance, and a sister ship to the *Fair Dawn* TT27, which joined the Tarbert fleet in 1970. Her wheelhouse was quite square looking in contrast with the other boats, a design which became popular in the late 1960s. She had no mainmast - and presumably no radio communication. The boat was bought into Tarbert in 1948, when her registration was changed from BF134 to TT140. Her new owner, Albert McDougall, pursued the ring-net method neighbouring the *Anne Marie* TT150 for a while. During the early 1950s the *Fairhavens* was a visitor to Whitby. In 1954, she was sold back to the north east and re-registered BF12.

The *Fairhavens* outside the *Mary Bain* TT35 and the *Silver Crest* TT75 beyond. (Valentines Collection, University of St Andrews)

TT141 MARGARITA

49.3 x 15.0 x 6.5 21.63 tons

This particular *Margarita* was 14 years older than the later *Margarita* TT26. She was another boat to come from William Weatherhead's yard at Cockenzie, built in 1934 as BA56 to replace the first 1927 Weatherhead *Margarita* BA117. At this time she was skippered by Jimmy Andrews, and ring-netted with the *Virginia* BA66. She later partnered the *Investor* BA58 during 1948. James (*Clyde*) McMillan brought her to Tarbert in the latter months of that year. During her time in the village she ring-netted with the *Monsoon* TT132 and the *Mary Bain* TT35. She reportedly fished at the Isle of Man as well as in the Clyde. In 1954, she was sold to the East Coast and re-registered FR15.

The bow of the *Margaret Ann II* TT16 is nearest the camera. Beyond are the *Silver Crest* TT75, the *Maireared* TT135, the *Mary Bain* TT35, the *Margarita* TT141, possibly the *Monsoon* TT132 and the *Marie Elspeth* CN116, which later became the *Silver Cloud* TT141.
(John Crawford Collection)

TT141
SILVER CLOUD/ AEOLUS

53.3 O/L
51.9 x 17.3 x 6.8   27.47 tons

The Fairlie Yacht Slip Ltd built this vessel in 1948 as the *Marie Elspeth* CN116 for Andrew Brown, of Campbeltown; she then spent several years on the Ayrshire coast as the *Silver Cloud*. Owned in Carradale for 12 years by Fred Brownie, registered CN267, she changed her home port to Tarbert in 1977 when bought by Richmond Murphy, who kept her for a year as TT141. The boat was then sold to Angus Johnson, who renamed her the *Aeolus*. She moved to Stornoway in 1980, where she was re-registered SY282, and later decommissioned. The boat was seen at the Lewis port in the early 1990s in a sad state, with broken planking and no wheelhouse.

The *Silver Cloud* at her home port of Carradale.
(John Crawford Collection)

The *Silver Cloud* later in her career, still with her original wheelhouse.
(Malcolm Stockdale Collection)

50.0 x 15.3 x 6.2   21.34 tons

William Weatherhead & Sons of Cockenzie built the *Mary Devereux* in 1933. Originally, she was named the *Golden Sheaf* BA195, based in the Ayrshire port of Maidens. In 1949 she was purchased by Tarbert skipper Duncan (*Mattha*) McDougall, who renamed the boat after his wife *Mary Devereux* and registered her TT148. She was a typical Weatherhead boat, with a distinct canoe stern and single top rubbing strip at the stern. She was later sold to Robbie McNeil (*Toga*), who ring-netted with the *Margaret Ann 11* TT16. The boat was sold in 1958 to be converted into a yacht at Leith and renamed the *Golden Sheaf*.

The *Mary Devereux* TT148 tied up outside the *Maireared* TT135, both showing off their
Weatherhead lines. They both came from Maidens as the *Golden Sheaf* BA195 and the
Maireared BA196. They were ring-net neighbours at that time.
(Author's Collection)

40.0 x 12.3 x 5.1 11.29 tons

James N Miller of St Monance built this boat in 1923. She was rarely seen in Tarbert
as she was based in Minard, owned and skippered by Duncan Munro. The rare
photograph shows her at Tarbert quay. Unusually, she had her registration number
painted lower down on her side under the single rubbing strip. Also noticeable is the
near vertical position of the brailer. She partnered the *Clan McNab* TT138 at the ring-
net. In 1938 her Tarbert registry closed and she was sold to Belfast. She was
converted for use as a pleasure boat, renamed the *Golden Plover*, and is still afloat.
The boat is currently owned by members of the 40+ Fishing Boat Association, and
bears her original Gaelic name *Sireadh* which means *seeking*.

The *Sireadh* TT150 berthed outside the boat believed to be the *Twin Sisters TT8* at Tarbert quay.
(Eric Irving Collection)

TT150 ANNE MARIE

54 .0 x 16.2 x 6.9 27.16 tons

One of the best-loved Tarbert boats was the *Ann Marie,* as she was part of the village fleet for 36 years. Another Weatherhead of Cockenzie boat, she was built at in 1948 for Hector McMillan of Tarbert, who is remembered in the village partly because he always wore a trilby hat. The boat was skippered by John (*Doods*) McDougall, a man also conspicuous by his choice of headwear, a naval type *cheesecutter* peaked cap, a rig favoured, too, by Dougie Bain of the *Village Belles.*

An 88hp Kelvin engine replaced the *Ann Marie's* original Mirrlees Blackstone 100hp engine, which vibrated excessively. Around 1961 she was re-engined again at Timbacraft of Shandon, with a 120hp Kelvin. During the 1960s, a new wheelhouse was installed at Dickie's boatyard, and the original fitted to the *King Fisher* TT55. The new wheelhouse was similar in design to those of the *Oak Lea* TT131 and the *Evelyn* TT58. This new addition, though bigger, was of a traditional style and did not spoil her appearance.

The *Evelyn* was her long-time ring-net neighbour and when that method ceased, both boats trawled for prawns and queen scallops. Among her crew were David Johnson, Archie Johnson and Robert McAllister, father of Neil who currently owns the *Catriona* TT79.

In the late 1960s, there was a considerable modification to the old style ring-net mast arrangement. Gone was the traditional diagonal style, and instead the masts were arranged with a vertically rising fixed mainmast set in the tabernacle. The mainmast supported the derrick base in a steel band and pin gooseneck affair, with the other end resting in a wooden crutch on the wheelhouse roof. The brailer pole was still pivoted from a heavy wooden deck block bolted at the after end of the hold coamings, angled upwards and lashed to the horizontal derrick. This set-up negated the need to manually hoist the mast for discharging the catch. This is clearly shown in the photograph, as is the tubular steel mizzenmast arrangement. However, she still looked a handsome boat.

She was later sold to Alexander and John Johnson, and decommissioned in 1984. The boat was not broken up, but sold - like the *Evelyn* TT58 - to Ireland. Research has been unable to tell me much about her present whereabouts. However, her name has possibly changed to the *Village Pride*, and she may have suffered some fire damage during her conversion.

The *Ann Marie* outside the green painted *Evelyn*. In the distance, the *Mary Devereux* and the *Mary Bain* are on the beach for their annual overhaul. (Author's Collection)

Above: A blue painted *Ann Marie*, still ring-netting, but with her masts in their later position. The owner and skipper can be seen on deck. (Author's Collection)
Below: *Ann Marie* discharging at Tarbert quay. (John Crawford Collection)

TT151 SILVER BIRCH

43.8 x 16.4 x 6.5   21.01 tons

The *Silver Birch* was another attractive boat from James Noble Ltd of Fraserburgh. She was built in 1947 as BF186 as shown on the photograph. After only two years she joined the Tarbert fleet and remained in the village as a ring-netter until her sale in 1954. She was a typical Noble vessel, if slightly shorter than some of her ring-net contemporaries, with a varnished hull and wheelhouse; she carried a mizzen sail when new. Willie McDougall and Donald McNeil owned her, and neighboured the *Polly Cook* TT85. She was sold to become CN6, but was unfortunately wrecked on the Post Rocks, west of Islay. She was replaced in Tarbert by the *May* TT48.

The *Silver Birch* in her original condition as a seine netter.
(Malcolm Stockdale Collection)

The *Silver Birch* on the beach for painting and varnishing.
(Author's Collection)

36.8 x 11.0 x 6.2   11.29 tons

John Fyfe of Port Banantyne built the *Peggy* in 1911 for Duncan and Sandy Johnson. She and her neighbour, the *Catherine* TT59 were known as the *Wee Pair* during the Second World War. According to the *Kist*, Issue 44, she used to moor between the Battery and Black's Coal-ree, along with around 10 other boats. Her time in Tarbert ended in 1950, when she was sold to Ireland.

*

TARBERT HARBOUR SCENES

A study in wheelhouse design featuring the *Village Maid II*, the *Village Belle III*, the *Maireared* and, outside, the *Margarita*. (Author's Collection)

The McAlpine's *Margarita* and *Maireared*, and the Jackson's *Village Belle III* and *Village Maid II*, with the *King Fisher* alongside the quay. (Author's Collection).

106

Two Donald Smith prints. The top shows the *Maireared* TT135, and the one below depicts the *Mhaighdean Mhara* UL276, referred to in the introduction. This boat was built by Noble of Fraserburgh in 1948, and later became the *Maggie McLean* OB30. These prints featured in calendars of the late 1950s and early 1960s. (Author's Collection)

Another Donald Smith print featuring the *Ann Marie* TT150.
(Author's Collection)

Above: A welcome visitor to Tarbert, the *Watchful* BA124, moored away from the quay to enable the crew to sleep in peace. She is now ashore at Ayr. Below: A ring-netter returns to Tarbert in 2003. Built by Alexander Noble of Girvan in 1966 the *Ribhinn Bhan* graces the harbour with the style of her classic lines. She is owned by Kenny and James McNab. (Author's Collection)

**Above: Dougie Bain holding the *Evelyn's* brailer pole during discharging work at Tarbert.
Below: Willie Dickson in the *Evelyn's* hold filling baskets with prime Clyde herring.
(John Crawford Collection*)***

APPENDIX I - THE BOAT BUILDERS

	NUMBER BUILT
William Weatherhead & Sons, Cockenzie	11
William Weatherhead & Sons, Eyemouth	1
Weatherhead & Blackie, Dunbar and Port Seton	2
James Noble (Fraserburgh) Ltd	11
James N Miller & Sons Ltd, St Monance	7
Walter Reekie, St Monance	5
Wilson Noble, Fraserburgh	2
Alexander Noble & Sons, Girvan	6
A M Dickie /Dickie of Tarbert Ltd	4
J & G Forbes, Sandhaven	4
George Forbes & Co, Peterhead	2
Thomas Fyfe, Tarbert	1
Archibald Leitch,Tarbert	1
Fairlie Yacht Slip Ltd	3
Matthew MacDougall, Portrigh, Carradale	1
John Fyfe, Port Banantyne	6
British Marine Motor Co, Whiteinch	1
Donald Munro, Blairmore	1
John Thompson, Ardrossan	2
Richard Irvin & Sons, Peterhead	1
John Stephen & Son,Banff	2
William&John Stephen, Banff	2
William Mahood, Portavogie	1
Robert Wylie, Campbeltown	1
J Adam & Sons, Gourock	1
Albert Palmer, Portavogie	1
Tommy Summers, Fraserburgh	1
Others / unknown	9

APPENDIX II - TARBERT FLEET LISTS

All vessels over 30 feet / 10 tons.
Smaller boats not listed.

TARBERT FLEET IN 1925-1930
Maggie McDougall TT2   *Village Maid* TT21   *Prime* TT27
Clan MacTavish TT68   *Mary Munro* TT71   *Willing Lad* TT83
Isa Johnson TT88   *Clan McNab* TT138   *Sireadh* TT150   *Peggy* TT334

TARBERT FLEET IN 1930-1935
Maggie McDougall TT2   *Village Maid* TT21   *Prime* TT27
Blossom TT30   *Seonaid* TT32   *Mary Bain* TT35
Osprey TT36   *Flying Fish* TT37   *Nellies* TT40
Smiling Morn TT50   *Clan MacTavish* TT68   *Mary Munro* TT71
Willing Lad TT83   *Isa Johnson* TT88   *Sireadh* TT150   *Peggy* TT334

TARBERT FLEET IN 1935-1940
Maggie McDougall TT2   *Village Maid* TT21   *Prime* TT27   *Blossom* TT30
Seonaid TT32   *Village Belle* TT34   *Mary Bain* TT35   *Osprey* TT36
Flying Fish TT37   *Nellies* TT40   *Smiling Morn* TT50   *Fionnaghal* TT65
Clan MacTavish TT68   *Sheila* TT70   *Mary Munro* TT71   *Willing Lad* TT83
Isa Johnson TT88   *Jessie* TT94   *Maireared* TT113   *Sireadh* TT150   *Peggy* TT334

TARBERT FLEET IN 1940-1945
Maggie McDougall TT2   *Nancy Glen* TT10   *Village Maid* TT21
Prime TT27   *Blossom* TT30   *Seonaid* TT32   *Village Belle* TT34
Mary Bain TT35   *Osprey* TT36   *Flying Fish* TT37
Fionnaghal TT65   *Mary Munro* TT71   *VillageBelle11* TT74
Willing Lad TT83   *Isa Johnson* TT88   *Jessie* TT94
Maireared TT113   *Little Flower* TT134   *Peggy* TT334

TARBERT FLEET IN 1945-50
Maggie McDougall TT2   *Nancy Glen* TT10   *Margaret Ann 11* TT16
Pride of the Clyde TT20   *Prime* TT27   *Golden Gleam* TT30   *Seonaid* TT32
Village Belle TT34   *Mary Bain* TT35   *Osprey* TT36   *Flying Fish* TT37
Nellies TT40   *Fionnaghal* TT65   *Mary Munro* TT71   *Village Belle11* TT74
Polly Cook TT85 *Jessie* TT94   *Maireared* TT113   *Frigate Bird* TT117
Oak Lea TT131   *Monsoon* TT132   *Maireared* TT135 *Fairhavens* TT140
Margarita TT141 *Mary Devereux* TT148   *Ann Marie* TT150   *Peggy* TT33

TARBERT FLEET IN 1950-1955
*Margaret Ann 11*TT16   *Pride of the Clyde* TT20   *Golden Gleam* TT30
Seonaid TT32   *Mary Bain* TT35   *Osprey* TT36   *Flying Fish* TT37
King Fisher TT55   *Fionnaghal* TT65   *Ranger* TT73   *Village Belle 11* TT74

Silver Crest TT75   *Polly Cook* TT85   *Jessie* TT94   *Scarbh* TT106
Titan TT110   *Maireared* TT113   *Frigate Bird* TT117   *Oak Lea* TT131
*Monsoon*TT132   *Maireared* TT135   *Fairhavens* TT140   *Margarita* TT141
Mary Devereux TT148   *Ann Marie* TT150   *Silver Birch* TT151

TARBERT FLEET IN 1955-1960
*Village Belle 111*TT34   *Mary Bain* TT35   *Osprey* TT36
May TT48   *Charlotte Ann* TT49   *King Fisher* TT55
Evelyn TT58   *Fionnaghal* TT65   *Ranger* TT73
Village Belle 11 TT74   *Silver Crest* TT75   *Dalriada* TT77
Maisie TT83   *Polly Cook* TT85   *Mhairead* TT104
Fionnaghal 11 TT106   *Titan* TT110   *Maireared* TT113
Frigate Bird TT117   *Oak Lea* TT131   *Maireared* TT135   *Fairhavens* TT140
Margarita TT141   *Mary Devereux* TT148   *Ann Marie* TT150

TARBERT FLEET IN 1960-1965
Our Lassie TT8   *Nancy Glen* (2) TT10   *Caledonia* TT17
Village Maid 11 TT25   *Margarita* TT26   *Village Belle 111* TT34   *Destiny* TT42
King Fisher TT55   *Maryeared* TT57   *Evelyn* TT58   *Ranger* TT73   *Silver Crest*
TT75   *Dalriada* TT77   *Maisie* TT83   *Polly Cook* TT85   *Mhairead* TT104
Fionnaghal 11 TT106   *Titan* TT110   *Frigate Bird* TT117   *Oak Lea* TT131
Maireared TT135   *Ann Marie* TT150

TARBERT FLEET IN 1965-1970
Endeavour TT2 *Tudor Rose* TT4   *Our Lassie* TT8   *Nancy Glen* (2) TT10
Caledonia TT17
Provider TT18   *Catriona/Harmony* TT24   *Village Maid 11*TT25   *Margarita* TT26
Catherine Ann TT31 *Village Belle 111* TT34   *Destiny* TT42   *King Fisher* TT55
Maryeared TT57   *Evelyn* TT58   *Golden West* TT72   *Ranger* TT73
Silver Crest TT75   *Dalriada* TT77   *Trustful 111* TT79   *Florentine* TT92
Boy Lorne TT94   *White Rose* TT100   *Fionnaghal 11* TT106   *Maireared* TT135
Ann Marie TT150

TARBERT FLEET IN 1970-1975
Endeavour TT2 *Our Lassie* TT8   *Nancy Glen* (2) TT10   *Caledonia* TT17
Provider TT18 *Catriona/Harmony* TT24   *Village Maid 11* TT25   *Margarita* TT26
Girl Maureen TT30   *Catherine Ann* TT31   *Pioneer* TT36   *Destiny* TT42
Utopia TT55   *Maryeared* TT57   *Evelyn* TT58   *Boy Ken* TT70
Village Belle 1V TT74   *Silver Crest* TT75   *Bellemar* TT76   *Dalriada* TT77   *Boy
David* TT78 *Taeping/Catriona* TT79 *Boy Lorne* TT94   *Sunbeam* TT117   *Ann
Marie* TT150

APPENDIX III - BOWS & STERNS

James N Miller & Sons Ltd, St Monance

James Noble (Fraserburgh) Ltd

W Weatherhead & Sons of Cockenzie

 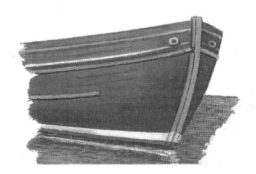

Walter Reekie of St Monance

ACKNOWLEDGEMENTS

I have already referred to people who have assisted during my research for this book. As previously stated, it is really a compilation of the vast knowledge of others put together in one publication. I sincerely hope I have not omitted anyone or used photographs without giving due credit. Where no photographic acknowledgement is given, the source is unknown, but is part of either John Crawford's or my own collection. The complete list of contributors is shown below.

Jessie Bain, Tarbert
Michael Craine, Onchan
John Crawford, Lochgilphead
Willie Dickson, Tarbert
Paul Gallagher, Tobermory
Jack Glover, East Ardsley
Freddy Gillies, Campbeltown/Isle of Gigha
Eric Irving, Ayr
Cilla Jackson, St Andrews University
Willie Jackson, Tarbert
Ann Logan, Oban
Douglas McAlpine, Tarbert
Peter McDougall, Tarbert
Arthur McFarlane, Tarbert
Mary McFarlane, Tarbert
James McNab, Tarbert
Nigel Musgrave, Conwy
National Maritime Museum
Alastair Parker, Perth
Robert Ross, Tarbert
Scottish Fisheries Museum, Anstruther
Malcolm Stockdale, Grimsby
Graham Ward, East Ardsley

Valentine images are reproduced by kind permission of the University of St Andrews Library, from those in my own collection published by James Valentine & Sons, Dundee.

BIBLIOGRAPHY

Life with the Coal Tar	Freddy Gillies
Tales from the Dawn Hunter	Freddy Gillies
The Ring-Net Fishermen	Angus Martin
Herring Fishermen of Kintyre and Ayrshire	Angus Martin
The North Herring Fishing	Angus Martin
My Captains	Tom Ralston
The Story of the Fishermen	Ronnie Johnson and Ann Thomas
Traditional Fishing Boats of Britain & Ireland	Michael Smylie
Fishing Boats	40+ Fishing Boat Association
The Kist 44 & 59	NHAS of Mid Argyll
Sea Breezes Vol 46 No 322	
The Motor Boat 1932	
Tarbert Fishing Boat Registers	
Tarbert Loch Fyne Guides	
Argyllshire Advertiser	